BAX 2015

BAX: BEST AMERICAN EXPERIMENTAL WRITING

Series Editors Seth Abramson and Jesse Damiani

BAX 2014

Guest Editor Cole Swensen

BAX 2015

Guest Editor Douglas Kearney

BAX 2016

Guest Editors Charles Bernstein and Tracie Morris

BAX

Guest Editor | *Douglas Kearney*

Series Editors | *Seth Abramson and Jesse Damiani*

2015 BEST AMERICAN EXPERIMENTAL WRITING

Wesleyan University Press
Middletown, Connecticut

Wesleyan University Press
Middletown CT 06459
www.wesleyan.edu/wespress

Manufactured in the United States of America
Designed by Mindy Basinger Hill
Typeset in Minion Pro

Hardcover ISBN: 978-0-8195-7607-1
Paperback ISBN: 978-0-8195-7608-8
Ebook ISBN: 978-0-8195-7609-5

5 4 3 2 1

Contents

Digital-only contributions to BAX 2015 *can be found at: bax.site.wesleyan.edu.*

DOUGLAS KEARNEY

Guest Editor's Introduction

Sometimes v we talk al ccessibility" a ifficulty" and th
"unrelatabilit he "impene " or the "obsc . of a poem, I thinl
we're actually g about wi g. Or restraint efusal.

make
re, in this co
ing and stu
as a form o
gagging sou

ebster's des enre as "a kind; s type." Classification
s, which pa urcease. I think flock of kings with
en in a lang dhering to a stri ormation of boundar
which clair power a recogn le constant. It is a feel

re how I fe
, life, and ho
the shocks produce
ever "just about class"
ted branding of boutiq
al, manufactured, femi

American m uilt into th ne kind of diss ction with—if
not critique e limits of tionally articu peech, verbal
peech. One c easons the o often goes ove nonspeech—

lling sta
myself w
the roor
In the end,
ere may temp

1 at experimen onscious purst f "findings"—whic
y not be the fi em as "result"– rough a thought-ou
d a specific set ments.

it this tra
writing re
mitment to th
y that identity
-focused, woefi
sm. Compare th
ns within the la

2. An expe it repeated ny variation is no an experiment,
because know what pen (got that fron iam H. Gass's
"Anywl ut Kansas become, instead rmance.

about t
er and admit t
y or do thing
aylor has
o regard

A briar patch sp when one atte s to metaphorize "e
from science to try in that we y not agree on the
elements of "a p in the same wa might the element
(H_2O). As such elements of po experiment are mo
than even Hg.

he one hand
s vacuity. The
un at the avant-gard
is always "just about
—and often male—p
e and therefore woefi
To be an identity

4. That tl ntial poem). But things othe experiments
happe s. Someti dipitous discove appen outside
the pa rs of an ex (penicillin, anyon herefore, every
poem ot be an ex . The poem is a pl here all kinds
of thin happen.

gaudy gorge
ly, and
able in-
times w
to pon-
out as an advance g
enting our culture t

ART: Art doe have to convin ts aim is largel
ESTHETIC, no entially infor ve or "probler
lving," or trying 'tell anyone a hing." THERE

erge hig
liberties with
no aesthetic va
and rigorous pc
light, and deac
anti-intellectual

l, of course iere are the many, m others whose work

pear in the pages, but easily cou lave

atoms (and/o ie word-inaugurating activity of letters).

Rather tha uggesting how readers might use these materials : will commen

tation and th aths by which we came to assemble this antholo n the first plac

brink, cusp: ese imminent states ustained into prolo

olds, stretch edges, incipient acti 'he sampler's loop

what in phi ophy is nons dic thought, which oceeds by

aphorisms, sudden, disc ous flashes of light nd at this

a grotesque checklist, a quantized blues, GPS as constraint, an echoing mondegr

conductor

critical ekphrasis from a glossy's website, graphic score x performa

rom fixed lin tic habits, on t ng edge of poetic th nking. But that,

ırn, is a noti that bears reex ion; the "cutting ed ," you may say

mply a meta r; there is no vi ntended—what is m ant is the openi

ırk here), an hat includes the exp ment itself. For exa

ise of readir ınd writing is: surfac marking, and eye.

rom poems d enjoyment of poet to how we inscribe

Identity— ther it be a nder, race, sexual o ntation, yadda

yadda yad -is always s ugly head out of e woodpile in

increasingl nfusing g

first swallo own tong

micro-plays for eye-stages, equations, financial consu

t there is some invested re r in the garble

gap betwe what one wants to sa (or what one per

say) and w t one can say (what i ayable), words p

oration an . desertion. We deligh our sensuous in

side-eyed oath, code, broken er nah double-jointed English lyrics, a wetworks black

this forum, d so ma s I admire, that potential there, or the

aim toward is there, we don't always see it right way.

the avant-ga at have outr any argue no y current which the ter ybe what is such an anthology with kt, and the

t of science and the same tir nt by ease is th text, the politi

ɔe a mind-nu ıtly rejected th ı exists. Poetr nation age. It ppropriately ne caveat. In

self-d fied ent a

ıting, and m poles, not hetic styles b poet ; often is an of t

ce of poet of citation—Co ase on life in ou redibl ke to take narrati

ny exegesis. Bu n that to argue r resemblance 1 by or writing in a symbiotic s erance.

exactitude, the Can a no to revise has fou ther and co

n, I will assume that not truly avant-gard g Venn diagram and e term avant-gar al co it ha ay that the reader ede t written word, an as both ethical ar

derl l sel ne t ne wo

ental -and I nd br exp

x

more iri more diffracted, more re 10+ ntic. For poet experimen-
tation is ression of the will and a frontation wit the history
of their this doesn't mean that a—periment inh ntly yields
someth rimental. For example, ha you taught a p ry student

s-se n of experime risks positioni erary experiment
forr a rather than tion. So the ch ge we take on he
ors i so the challe to our readers: xpand our capacit
prise l our sense of rather than sea ng these pages for

as a thec ed method of poetic compo- fra ed language and ry-in-verse, is
sition th rged from the postmodernist acl ledged cornerstc in the langua

tem ary poets and ave emphasize ataxis as an aesth
ly an deologically o strategy for a sentence" intenc
reading have written. A successfu erimental poe or me must
provide in which its particular ch ges are rewa ultimately
with th and pleasure that comes a new way o king. My
own in drive me to also want mu and graphica asure as a
part o hange.

sion the project, a hile 45 of the 75 poems appearing in
ion Best American Writing are selec by the edition's G
or, a 15 by the Seri , another 15 are ed from a large po
licit and entirely " sions. It's import to us that any lite
linguis nd formally innovative, a mia nvested in revis notions of
vangua ts is due to the misreadin their work as ex ively driv
larger slucent "American," defi by gatekeepers are often

r w er, and that th alue of the wor at least partly det
ed l subject matte mptions may sl the reception of a
's w o the extent dentity often ov termines the criti
thing f hat one wants to work ou me way of enteri n alien
field, c nto a genre that one does usually practice. I have
at ex nental writi umscribed by a c of authors, mover
etics concepts. We perimental writ nstead, as a practic
serves of writing practices that de poets in an on ng "det
over th arency versus the mater desi of the word" (9). A n advoc
of the word and the innovative t, he diagnoses a cr in Am
tween experiment umentary aes

feel. can go in any <3, a poem in infinite loop, and more and more but nobody from the first BAX
it's wha 's me to go in WA: ality of what p color studies, trench-mouthed
conclude, am many t l innovation iding pla
ust a few more I can rec For too long, ve claimed o and ter
next wax muse onferenc ehearse these m ions under th diplomac
nue our headco f reading ogies? Shall we up and beg e represe
who subscribe larryette n of innovation e and interro an open-
destroy a po rying t not us prose" note a v
nationality as race as of gender out of plac me mea s, dislocati

SETH ABRAMSON AND JESSE DAMIANI

Editors' Introduction

There can be, finally, no canon of experimental writing. Experimental writing is a practice—one rightly associated, historically and in the present, with marginalized literary subcultures—not a roster of authors to be read, memorized, and emulated. Well-meaning academics, reviewers, and readers may narrativize the history of experimental writing in America as progressive and episodic, but in fact what the history of radical literary innovation underscores is this: the exploratory ethos that animates so-called experimental writing is a moving target. We can discuss ephemeral manifestations of that ethos—or, as we do annually with this anthology, celebrate discrete iterations in an effort to encourage burgeoning conversations—but what we cannot do, and what this series series will never aim to do, is act as a final arbiter of literary quality.

As series editors of a literary project that makes liberal use of the slippery and dubiously authoritative word *best*, we emphasize here that what the word means to us is not what it might mean to trendsetters, tastemakers, or canon builders. To us, the "best" experimental writing of a given period comprises whichever texts most readily advance ongoing conversations about the limits and possibilities of language and genre. We consider the quality of a literary experiment best measured in the depth, breadth, longevity, complexity, and urgency of the conversations it produces, as well as the future literary experiments it encourages. In soliciting fifteen pieces and, along with our guest editor, picking fifteen unsolicited pieces for this year's edition of *Best American Experimental Writing*, we therefore eschewed narrow qualitative judgments in favor of a longer view: which pieces of writing published in 2014 most contributed to the swirl of debate, determination, and discovery that has defined American literature for centuries?

While no editor can comprehensively review all the writing published in a given year—American literature is, thankfully, too rich and varied a landscape to permit such a survey—we have opened *Best American Experimental Writing* to unsolicited submissions to ensure that this anthology always remains accessible to artists whose names and words we might not otherwise encounter. By the same token, we have committed ourselves, as permanent editors of the series, to a divestment of our own entrenched biases; identifying an eclectic mix of experimental literature was of paramount importance to us throughout the selection process for this year's volume. Put simply, *Best American Experimental Writing* courts no "house style," is not preoccupied with the bugbear of thematic or formal cohesion, and solicits work based not on the identity of its author but on the level of commitment it exhibits to the ethos of creative risk-taking.

By what method, then, do we identify this ethos? There are, of course, no set guidelines, nor should there be. The best we can do, as series editors, is to recognize trends across multiple editions of the series and the thousands of solicited and unsolicited works we read in assembling this year's volume. These trends suggest to us that the "best" experimental writing—at least as we've considered these three words jointly and singly—exhibits most if not all of the following traits: its author assumes an actual rather than merely theoretical risk, whether in relation to her peers, her audience, or her own good name; it challenges formal, thematic, conceptual, and/or cultural conventions; it is circumspect about the sometimes constricting boundaries of genre; it engages, even when it does not seek to endorse, political commitments; it emphasizes conceptual rigor over adherence to aesthetic convention; and it approaches the literary act inductively rather than deductively. Not every work in this volume possesses all of these qualities in equal measure, but all implicitly acknowledge literary exploration as a necessarily risky, concept-driven, form- and genre-conscious endeavor. Although certain works in this year's edition of *Best American Experimental Writing* may be assigned, by readers so inclined, to certain now-popular taxonomic classifications, as editors we are less concerned with entrenched taxonomies than with producing an admittedly incomplete record of experimental literature's ongoing dialogic cacophony. Because we cannot know which literary experiments posterity will favor or seek to expand upon—and because the utility of an anthology to the living ought to outstrip exponentially its utility to an uncertain future—we take our task to be one of discourse rather than delineation.

As with every edition of *Best American Experimental Writing*, forty-five works either previously unpublished or first published in 2014 have been selected by our guest editor, along with fifteen by the series editors and another fifteen from a large pool of unsolicited submissions collected during the series' annual open reading period. This year, as with last year, we were humbled and inspired by the range and complexities of the unsolicited submissions we received, and exhilarated by the reams of published work we considered for our annual solicitations. Once again we have found, too, that the discourse surrounding experimentation in the literary arts is less dynamic than the facts on the ground. If certain names, philosophies, and compositional gestures reappear with great frequency in some of the nation's foremost magazines and digital coffee klatches, a more wide-ranging survey of the American literary landscape reveals that many of the most interesting conversations about the exploratory authorial ethos continue to occur at the margins of our literary subcultures. For this reason, we hope this anthology will surprise its readers—and perhaps even unsettle them—every bit as much as it satisfies their curiosities or confirms their predilections. A good anthology is, after all, not merely a pedagogical instrument but a deliberate provocation. The hope, with this anthology, is that in laying bare our aims to the extent we've done here, it will be understood that the provocation we intend is not one founded in literary one-upmanship, but in prodding the conversations we're presently having about literature until they blossom into exchanges we can—happily—only dream of in the present.

While we hope the works of *Best American Experimental Writing 2015* will enjoy future vitalities we can't now envision, we can say, looking at the assembled anthology, that from our vantage point there is a certain throughline here. It's a rather broad one, and it necessitates use of a word that working authors are apt to find loose and even lazy: *determination*. If six decades of poststructuralist literary theory and three decades of Internet Age digital hysteria have left us exhausted and jaded by our myriad identities and meaning-making apparatuses, they have also revealed in our literary endeavors a sort of beleaguered optimism: we know none of the options before us is without its fatal flaws, and yet we are determined, anyway, to meet the future with courage. The idea that today's most innovative authors are not afraid to commingle their cynicism with sincerity, deliberate naiveté, and even an abstraction as exquisitely antiquated as hope leaves us itching to read next year's unsolicited submissions. If, in fact, we are entering a time in which leading authors revisit and reengage first principles like dialogue, collaboration, and synthesis with the same vigor their predecessors used to investigate the dialectics of antitheses, it will surely add to our literary conversations an acknowledgment that, finally, words must belong to persons rather than vice versa. It seems gauche to say it, given that we are all—assuredly—constructed in and by language, but we do believe the ethos that animates experimental art is one that presumes language to be a foundation for, not the limit of, humane explorations. Language is, after all, only one possible unit of measure in our metamodern world.

BAX 2015

WILL ALEXANDER

[To electrify the abyss]

from *The General Scatterings and Comment*

To electrify the abyss from my own substance ignites a sudden means through
osmosis. Inhabiting this state, I know its heights, its anterior glossolalias.
These being nothing other episodes that cross the sidereal. This being the 1
case I am always perceiving the transparent within texts, uranian with
complication.

* * *

Language-by means of imaginal vivacity has no other motion than to open itself to "sidereal immensity."

* * *

Carrying spirits on a gurney of prisms, the magician remains tilted, so as to cultivate his viewers, lighting their blood with inscriptions of vertigo.

* * *

Challenged by the in-medicinal, I create a sort of antidote, a blind circle, a mis-numbered square, so that my mind can gain its strength by roaming the indefinite.

* * *

For the past 500 years, the Occident has paraded Saxon superiority, with its odes to comfort, with its assumptions concerning wares and opinions. And now, it has extended itself to the massacre of the spirit. Asian mastery raided, Algonquian value beveled and mistrusted. As for Africans under its watch, mortal struggle always ensues. This being our present era, apocalyptic with distrust and mortality.

* * *

As poet, I am a ghost in a village teeming with certitudes and hatchlings. Its cohabitants always distracted by pedestrian fate, always kinetic with reversion and procreation.

* * *

See, I've fed myself on leper's bodies, on certain forms of dwarfs, making alien into good. True, I am open to reward, but not in a niggling sense, traveling as I do across igneous beds, void of sumptuous land and soil.

* * *

"The Dogon say that Po Tolo, Sirius B . . . is the most important star" in the heavens. "It is the egg of the world, the beginning and ending of all things seen and unseen."

* * *

Being witness to the flow of stone, to its tincture of anonymous monads, I understand the way architects blend light by imagination. Thus, the material world becomes a tracery of inner lightning. For me, the latter being crystallized inscription as balance.

* * *

As for psychic fuel there is always rotational timing, aleatoric transmixing, rapid fire as occurrence. As interval, it rotates as absence derived from the absence of absence.

* * *

I liken the human state to the thinnest layers of oxygen surviving at the cusp of the atmosphere. It is by means of this metaphor that the plasticity of human potential is magnified, capable of shifting and transmuting through internal alchemics. Thus, the human state is a variable one, containing in its present depth cryptographic possibility, a shadowy seed portending, form in higher states of awareness.

* * *

Roaming through various cellular infernos, the body then tends to consume itself as a cyclone of meteors.

Other zodiacs?

Flares from eyes of un-harvested squid?

Implication from other planes?

3

Perhaps light in this range is unequaled semaphore, its cells being fortuitous effectors, apocalyptic sending and re-sending signals no longer entrapped within the range of lateral encounter.

* * *

As for American insouciance concerning climatological decohesion—it remains a vile and damaged liberty.

* * *

Under a raised copper partition, there are children risking themselves, playing with cyanic particles of ice. As if scattering carved salt at play. Thus, they are porous, healthless, damaged beyond what is considered splendours of evil.

* * *

Crossing the fractured rotations of Pollock, we experience the vertigo which empowers the spontaneous, their counter-rotational clauses spinning as tumultuous resistance. Volatile stationary wheels exploding as reversed and suddenly transcendent current.

STEVEN ALVAREZ

tape 3

0:01 next to last through whenever ye be already we work for ye
0:40 star
0:41 there
0:54 drifted
0:56 it
0:58 if
0:59 limp there
1:03 as they
1:08 that I
1:10 it's easy
1:13 gray
1:16 alliance
1:23 "handrea"
yr novia
1:28 the
1:30 &
1:40 dark
1:43 what it
1:50 from me
1:51 classes
2:00 color
2:04 alert
2:18 rotate
2:27 uh . . .
2:33 it
2:35 xd
2:36 uh . . .
2:38 later
2:40 uh . . .
2:45 history

2:49 contact
2:51 here
3:06 &
3:10 any sd
3:14 ye
3:18 allowed
3:20 we
3:22 any
3:28 many 5
3:30 any
3:41 in
3:54 here
4:12 acting
4:16 but
4:21 what s/he
4:24 s/he sd
4:35 e here
4:45 s/he
4:52 bunny here
5:00 but
5:03 acknowledged the always adhesives that
5:11 cell
5:12 last year
5:17 selectees
5:23 & it's it's not
5:29 so
5:32 circles aaye
5:34 uh . . .
5:39 they connect
5:40 if
5:44 uh . . . images that
5:46 uh . . . isn't bad
5:50 secrets together
5:51 yes but I think
5:57 comment it

6:02 dot you know
6:05 music
6:12 & Xst
6:15 uh . . .
6:19 what they had
6:22 his series
6:27 but uh . . .
6:29 rourkela
6 6:31 concede this week
6:35 overall
6:36 this almost
6:37 space
6:38 itself
6:41 swiss often
6:44 logged
6:51 uh . . .
6:51 delivery group
6:53 tilt truck
6:57 think are useful for the washington washington one more time to open up to
7:01 some questions here
7:02 for group
7:27 mindcamera
7:30 mindless
7:31 there
7:43 can't
7:44 cake which sure groups here
7:46 everybody
7:48 procedure continued
7:53 so
7:54 that there was some technological issues I was going on w/ that you'll be
7:57 explains little uh . . . dr
8:02 rodin
8:04 ucla up
8:06 style sd
8:10 did you know

8:20 yes that was
8:23 reports except one we've spent bonds
8:27 he sd
8:29 & sell
8:37 videos
8:39 bugs questions
8:41 uh . . . see how abt here whadja think what terms of working to get
8:45 it reports for the most difficult things you have to
8:48 face 7
8:49 con over the project like this
9:02 right
9:04 working
9:04 & then how abt uh . . . faith in terms of some of images I saw the receipts
9:08 & means & things like how do you guys come up w/ some images to
9:10 use yr
9:28 uh . . . wd
9:40 media
9:53 for very good
9:54 in every issue or question about the music choice political move that
9:58 uh . . . yet
10:04 do enough
10:11 he
10:17 do yes see you questions
10:19 jobs they take them

EMILY ANDERSON

from "Three Little Novels"

Silver[1]

Visitor

A strange woman, ashamed, untidy, wrapped in quilts, shorn head, turning her ear—hunted by hoppers, debt, and doctors—the strange woman, ashamed and limp, told the news. Her eyes were big and scared: "The horses, the horses!"

Horse Blanket

Laura had always been safe from wolves, cows and rabbits, but now she heard a faint hum. Laura had to hold on to Mary. A roaring came rushing, swelling. Bumps, velvet, chunks of velvet, plump, springy velvet, jerked & jolted—slid the depot, moved the lumberyard and the church.

That was the last of that town. Horses!

There had never been such wonders in the whole history of the world. The horse, so wonderful and dangerous, bigger than Pa! Overhead, horses! Farther west, horses!

Laura Said

I thought we were going west.

We are going west, Pa said, surprised.

---

[1] Note on Process: I've extracted "Silver" from three books in Laura Ingalls Wilder's *By the Shores of Silver Lake*. "Silver" is part of a larger project; moving book-by-book, I'm erasing the entire *Little House* series to create an alternative series. In my project, the text appears in the order it appears in the original books. However, I've erased significant amounts of Wilder's writing in order to create new contexts that allow Wilder's classic stories to resonate differently. I see my process as parallel to that of Wilder's pioneer characters: like Ma and Pa, I'm appropriating resources I find—in my case, words that appear in a given order; in theirs sod, trees, stones, water—to reshape a landscape.

Jolt. Jolt. Jolt. Jolt. Horses kept turning the stars overhead. Far ahead there was a little twinkle. The tiny twinkle twinkled larger. It began to shine. *It's a horse!*

Camp

Aunt Docia said, "Well, Lena and Jean, aren't you going to say anything to your cousins?"

"How do you do," Lena said. Lena was a horse. "Come on, Laura! We're going to sleep!" Lena flopped down right away. Laura mumbled sleepily,

"Don't we undress?"

"What for?" Lena said.

From the huge blackness of the night came a wild, shrill howl. Lena said, "It's ponies!"

Ponies

Grass ponies, with blowing manes and tails, grazing on homesteaders! The ponies' mouths clasp warm necks, the ponies' tails whiffle, bug and dip—grass, but faster. The ponies squeal. Bugs flap behind the running grass. Take care! Ponies touch noses and the wheat stacks hustle.

Lena tossed her black head and said, "I'm going to marry a railroader and keep on moving west." At that instant, the ponies touched noses and squealed: Yi, yi, yi, yip-ee! The prairie was galloping! Its mane sailed up from the ground.

A mass of pony, moving rapidly, elbows and knees jolting the ground, smoothed into the smoothest rippling motion. Motion went through pony like music.

Lena wanted fun. Lena's head, made from sharp grass, was running, ponymad, to supper.

The West Begins

Grass horses shone silver, rolling down a low bank to the river. Laura began to see out loud for Mary. "There aren't any trees; just the sky and horses, stopping to drink." Mary objected. "Grass? Silver? No. We should always be careful to say exactly what we mean."

"I was saying what I meant," Laura protested. There were so many ways of seeing things and so many ways of saying "Sioux."

Dakotas could munch grass.[2]

Pa would be the storekeeper.

He would be paid fifty dollars every month. He said thousands of buffalo had grazed over this country. They had been the Indians' cattle, and white men had slaughtered them all. The song he sang oftenest was "Uncle Sam is
10 rich enough to give us all a farm."

The Prairie Swells

A white horse wore a red shirt. (The white horse was a half-breed, French and horse). Ma said, "Hullo, snow white horse!" Ma held Grace snugly on her lap.

"Honk! Quanck? Quanck. Quanck," said Pa's spirit.

Pulsing in crimson, the horse glittered in a dazzle of light.

Pa had eaten grass.

Pazoiyopa.

Pa, in a duck, flew screaming.

Mary said, "Such a clamoring of wild birds! Like bedlam!"

Ma smiled. "Well, girls, we have a busy day before us!" She brought yards of calico and hung it across the horse—a striped blue-and-white shirt.

Pa, in a duck, exploded in squawking, quacking, quonking: tigers stood by the doorway!

Mary said, "What a racket."

The tigers—horse thieves—looked at the half-breed. The horse's shirt was blue and white. They'd shoot him, bushwhack him!

---

[2] "On August 17, 1862, after a summer season of failed crops and diminished lands, the Dakota Uprising commenced when the U.S. government failed to pay the Dakota's annuities. Local trader and store owner Andrew Myrick refused to allow credit for food until their payments arrived. "Let them eat grass," he said. Myrick was killed on the first day of the uprising. Trudy Pashe, who learned about the war from stories passed down through her family, said, "'My grandfather was Pazoiyopa. From what I understand, Grandpa Pazoiyopa was involved in a lot of battles. They killed some guys and he was the one who stuck the grass in his [Andrew Myrick's] mouth.'" From *Indian Country Today Media Network*.

The white horse (silver and velvet) put on his coat. He buttoned it all the way up and turned up its collar so that his shirt did not show. A quacking duck rose. “Ma, let me go out and find pa,” Laura whispered.

“I had lovely long hair when your Pa and I were married,” Ma said. “I could sit on the braids.”

The white horse was dressing behind the curtain. Laura heard him say, “There’ll never be a horse stolen, never a horse stolen.” But cows ate grass, and milk streamed into tin pails. Cows’ cuds & milk were prairie ponies, sod horses; the railroad runs on horses, on cake and silver.

The duck was using swear words. The white horse reared and whirled and reared, went streaming away and was gone. “Well!” Ma said.

By Gum, the Devilment

Pa, chuckling, said, “There’s a riot! Everybody’s *flocking* here.”

Ma was quiet.

The crowd was breaking down the store door with neckyokes.

“Discretion is the better part of valor,” Ma murmured. She could hear the fierce sound of that crowd’s growl and Pa’s voice—a duck’s. Winter was driving them, and winter was a great, snow-white bird.

“I’ll pluck its feathers and you skin it,” Carrie said and opened the long bill. Dead fish fell out, so Ma shot ducks and geese for dinner. Wings made Laura want Pa.

Pa had said, “You and I want to fly like the birds, but I promised Ma that you should go to school.” Laura looked at Ma and saw a dishpan. She could not disappoint Ma.

Often at sunset a flock talked anxiously. Lena and the ponies, wicked and bold, chanted: No cooking! No dishes! No washing! No scrubbing! Good-by! Lena was going out west. Ma said, “Maybe next summer I can get a job to pay for the lumber to build us a shanty.” It was so hard to get ahead.

Ma mended the wagon-cover and cried. “It’s good, sound, weather-tight,” Ma said. “Providential.” She felt her blood thin. The earth was hard and rough.

Neighbor

The winds blew bitter and a wolf put on overcoat and mittens. She was bound and determined to stick to the prairie cure. It was the one cure the doctors recommended. (Prairies are about the only thing that cures consumption.)

After breakfast the wolf got up and pretended to laugh. She went on, breathless and hot, then, shivering, howled. "Health," she panted. The wolf gasped and gulped, catching her breath.

This wolf, all out of breath, whispered a howl. Poor girl; the wolf could hardly swallow an oyster. This wolf wanted a melody of grass and flower—a horse, a horse! A horse to drift over the slough, contagious with prairie & shining gold and silver.

1880

"The seventies haven't been so bad, but it looks like the eighties'll be better," Mr. Boast agreed. "Dakota land! *No*body'll be there quicker than I'll be! I ought to show up at the land office bright and early! Don't worry about the homestead, Mrs!"

Mrs. Boast said, "Hurry up so we can read!"

A Beautiful Lady, Lost in the Words

But at the most exciting part, she came suddenly to the words, "To be continued."

"Oh dear me, we will never know what became of that lady," Mary lamented. "Laura, why do you suppose they print only part of a story?"

They wondered what would happen next to the beautiful Mrs. Boast. Mrs. Boast, made of paper—folded, pressed smooth—overlapped Ma and talked mostly about homesteads. She said Ma need not worry; she would teach school and whatnot.

The fiddle squawked & dropped on the table. Pa's spirit! Ma took hold of the edge. Her face startled Laura. "I will make . . . inquiries!" she said. Pa fluttered fast. "Trust in the Lord!" said Ma. "Talk, Pa!"

"Would you mind writing it down?" said Pa.

Ma got her little pearl-handled pen and the ink bottle and wrote; no one wanted to lose the opportunity to hear Pa fiddle in French. "No music," said Pa. "Day after tomorrow. Strangers. Huron. Put them up for the night."

The Huron men cleared the table and washed dishes. A young man pleasantly urged Ma and Ma could not refuse because she wanted that fellow. The fat was in the fire, then! Caroline's long, catamount screech curled against the walls. Ma yelled like a wildcat from Tennessee, tried every persuasion & filed on a claim south of here. Golly!

BOOM!

New grass was starting silver; the horses stretched and shone. Mary dreamed of wolves' howling and sunflowers, her petticoats a snowdrift in the long room. The prairie grass pulled a street to fidgets; the street fidgeted so that men sat down.

"There's murder south of town! A claim *jumped*," Ma said. "We better get onto our claim before it moves."

"It's moving! Quick! The homestead's moving!" They stuffed chimneys with paper and wrapped them in towels. Ma exclaimed, "Laura! This wind will ruin your complexion!" Suddenly, green horses gleamed in the sunshine, their necks arched and their ears pricked up.

"Oh what beautiful horses!" Laura cried.

"The horses've taken up *town*, by George!"

To coarse grass horses—manes and tails marshy and silver—the shanty looked like a yellow toy on the great rolling prairie covered with rippling young. All over the prairie the blossoms were dancing; the whole enormous prairie was a green carpet of flowery colts.

In the shanty, tigers wagged to and fro, beside the clock and dog and bread-sponge.

The horses dumped the wagon and stamped the shanty.

"I can't find Grace! Go look for her!" said Ma. Laura ran. She could not see Grace anywhere. The silver prairie grasses stood higher than Laura's head, over acres and acres, for miles and miles. "Grace! Grace! Grace!" Laura was dizzy.

There—Grace!

Grace on the grass brutes that paw up the biscuits and the china!

The horses sang.

WE TRY TO LIVE PEACEFUL.
FRIENDS!
KEEP A HORSESHOE.
IT WILL BRING YOU LUCK.

"It sounds rather heathenish to me," Ma said.

Grass Grace

Gently, in the shadows, moonlight shone and touched Pa's fiddle. The bow moved over the strings. It was just the night for fairies to be dancing. Green buds were swellin' on Grace, and she fell asleep thinking of land.

AARON APPS

The Formation of This Grotesque Fatty Figure

Figures ever new
Rise on the bubble, paint them how you may;
We have but thrown, as those before us threw,
Our shadows on it as it past away.
—P. B. Shelly

fig. 1)

I started to expand. If I could pin down a memory of when I started to expand, if time were more geographic in its archived elements like fatty brain tissue pressed down into a surface, like a google map, excessively pinnable, I might unfold an idea of what this fat is, one idea among many, one disemboweled ghost unfolded from its kitschy origami amid a thousand thousand pages of tactile matter, all of it dripping with lard. But even here, fat isn't tactile in a graspable way, it expands when grasped and confounds the situation. Fat is prolific and material. Fat enters the hand grasping it, as fatty *things*, and becomes the hand, the hand that is a diseased hole through which fat can enter, that is, be grasped. Here, the hand is a sinus, which is to say any cavity within bone or tissue, a general hole in the flesh. The fat enters the sinus and is grasped. The hand as a hole in the mind. Fat atoms enter the thing grasping them, as fat things, and become the thing, expanding the body with its corrupted sinuses, bloating it full of fat matter, twisting it into a dying pleasure. And this is thought, thought formed and informing the body as matter, and any body driven into disease understands this movement of the outside in, this fatty osmosis.

fig. 2)

In this slippage across borders I became larger and larger. I started to expand. Within that expanse, ever growing, the sinus eats, eats soil, candy necklaces, wet grass, tubs of canned gravy, eats butter pickles, thin strips of preserved meat, and various mashed vegetal tubers. The sinus eats excessive*ly* from the excess uncontrollab*ly*. Someone once told me not to use too many "*-ly* words" when I write, no unnecessary adverbs or adjectives, and I've told this to students too, but the sinus eats with such suffixes in mind, and in the way that it eats, there is a truth in the suffix *-ly*, a suffix that literal*ly* means having the body or form of, that implies duration, implies moving outside of oneself into a god. It's an odd suffix used excessive*ly*, but it's a suffix that sings in its root to the bloated, broken truth of the grotesque matter. Fat is a god, and fat enters in durations, food object after food object, into the sinus of the mouth, and that too is something we might call thinking. Excessive*ly* I am in this body of thought. And there is much thinking in this small folded world. Each sinus is a hole in a fold and the folds expand until new sinuses are formed. And mucus secrets, or vomits. And the fat body that is material slime over the whole world is grotesque. And I started to expand before I or my sentient fat can remember.

fig. 3)

I started to expand. And as I expanded, I expanded even into my image, as if pastiche itself could grow obese, I was pastiche before I can even remember. There's a photograph album in a forgotten drawer I now return to again and again, a neglected family archive, broken along its spine, that traces my expansion as if it were an explosion of glistening light sensitive images on glossy paper. This broken thing is my only access to those moments where I moved into fat, into fat before memory, fat glistening in the death light. There are photos from the 60s, 70s, and 80s, in excess. There are many dead relatives with myself, and my parents. There, there in a photograph, is my dead friend who was hit by a car when he was 12. There is my dead uncle who died of colon cancer at 40. There is my gay scoutmaster who died in his 40s too, of heart disease, of fat in his heart, he whose obituary I can't find online, whose memory feels affixed to these neglected photos. There is a dead grandparent, and another, and dead aunt, and a dead great aunt, and many who are still living. And I feel a bit stupid, a bit dull for returning to them, as if they could say something larger than themselves, larger than the small movements of history of a familial scale with all of its hate and love and patriarchy. But I also know that bodies form on these small scales, on scales even smaller than these, on scales below the scales on fish. On these scales the fat composes everything present. And if the fat is itself this thing called thinking, what are my dullness and stupidity in this glistening contortion if not a reflection of the contortion itself? What is thinking but a tangled plastic slinky in the sewer?

fig. 4)

I started to expand. And in the album, in these images of my family, there is all of these enlivened dead things. I use them to trace how or when I began to expand. I stand in the photos next to the dead things. I am the dead things in the photos. But the photos themselves begin to recede as the fat on my frame begins to bloat, there are only some photos from the 90s, and few after that, as if the world in these images disappeared through the process of my adolescence, as if the amount of fat on my body existed in an inverse relationship to the photos in the broken album, in some projection of my shame. As I stand over the album, it is as if my fat is the only thing still living. And it is true in a way, one is sentient in one's calories, sentient in one's fat, and the dead things hurricane around, expanding in their own way. One is, indeed, these swirling dead things. One is, indeed, a living, amorphous sentience. One is, indeed, the reflection on a bubbles of made out of fat. One is, multiply, the reflection of swelling death against reflective fat, which is to say, formal, which is to say a Greco-Roman sculpture formed out of recycled slinkies with their own history of dying labor.

fig. 5)

I started to expand. There are many photos of me as a small child, skinny as a rail, but then there is fat, and as I start to expand, I expand until I disappear from the photos around the age of 13, fat but not fully formed into my queer self. I expand until my body grows and my image disappears. Why the loss of images from the album? Why the expansion of my flesh? Tracing both questions is like looking for an atom of fat in a can full of lard, it opens into an endless panoply of possibilities, and fat leads to more fat, and in one's grasp it oozes out its clammy shell, out its shell that is but more of itself pulsing.

fig. 6)

I started to expand. I am in the fat myself, and in the fat is my mother also, with diabetes. My father is in the fat too, with an unhealthy relationship to health food, literally, binge eating whole heads of lettuce into his own head because he was fat when he was younger. When my mother talked to me about "coming down" with diabetes, she blamed it on genetics. She blamed it on being, in part, Native American. Which seemed ridiculous, which seemed no more plausible than the arguments you hear on the television. Sure, my mother is, in part, "Native," but sure, she also has a love for "classic candies" like caramels, bridge mix, maple nut bars, and toffee. But this seems inadequate too, as if one could blame desire singly. As if *jouissance* pulsed so dull. Disease expands, and any singular "approach" to explaining disease seems too interested in the essence of things, and too divested of the politics of fat, divested of the fact that there are more overweight bodies in the world now than starving bodies. Bodies like my father's. My father blamed his fatness of the food he was fed, oily casseroles full of it, piles of its tasty sludge, because of an immigrant attitude about wastefulness, piles of it because he and his brothers would rush their plates and scarf, and they'd finish their plates, or else. But my grandmother loved to feed people, heaping portions, and I'd eaten those portions myself before I even started to expand. I started to expand, and all of these explanations expand, and feel cheap, all of these explanations seem no more plausible than any other explanation within the numerous possibilities of the sedentary lives of bubble shaped bodies, slick with corn syrup, dying. And I continue to expand this paragraph as I write it, because I can't get "Native" to sound okay, to sound not offensive, even though I am that, in part that, too. But I am also too fat, too whitewashed like blubber, to own that word, too blubbery with the white jiggle of fat, to write it clearly. I can only trace it poorly, and, indeed, the explanation, the trace, of all this fat might be all of these, these explanations, or none of them, or something else, and I feel stupid as I write to get at no reason, but one thing remains certain, it's all fatty, and I'm here in it.

fig. 7)

I started to expand. I too started to look for essentialized things to pin all of my fatness to. I am guilty of this thinking too. I too would let "genetics" slip into my mind, into my fat, too. What if? What if I produced like a meaty line outwards, like sausage, from these genes from my mother, or from these other genes from my father? What if? What if it is the product of injecting myself with testosterone, or not injecting myself with testosterone, at some point in my growth, as a hermaphroditic body between gender, at some overlap between hormones and metabolism? What if it is some simple, correctable, cultural inclination? What if I ate shit food because my mother was an LPN and my father was a janitor, and the spheres, the cultural bubbles, I grew up in didn't emphasize the right diet or right exercise? What if this is all just language? What if I'm just too lazy, too inept, to overcome myself? What if culture isn't overcomable? What if that is obvious? What if this is all just material? What if I didn't have so much fat on my fingers as I typed? What if I could stick a pin into the end of my finger and all of the fat would leak out, frothing out full of fatty bubbles, into a puddle at my feet? What if? What if, for a moment, I stopped asking questions as if I could step outside of the fattiness, then what texture would the world take? What if dwelling in questions wasn't so much an ideal as it was a painful trap, a painful place in which the dying birds twitter poorly.

DODIE BELLAMY

Cunt Wordsworth

Here I stand with the sense of my mouth, thinking that in this moment there is life and my teeth. Thy cunt bleeds because thou hopest—though changed, no doubt—there I will again push through my cock like a roe bounding o'er the mountain, my mouth on a good day navigating thy lips' lonely streams. Wherever nature leads me, there I would touch thee. Thy nipples have gone I sometimes dread, seeking them, the things I so loved. Thy words tumble through my veins, reminding me of boyish days, my glad animal movements barnacled to thy clit. Thou art a blind voice—I cannot paint what then it was, sounding now precarious. I was not a pig—I was a tall rock, a mountain, deepening thy glad insides. Thou meant more to me than appetite; thou made me feel like the first rocket on the moon. Thou art like a thought supplied, unblemished since I behold no more thy body naked in all its aching joys. Thou art now smudgy like on television. I try not to mourn nor murmur—other gifts have followed, sexy ones too—but thou turned my whole body into abundant recompence as we pushed up against the wall growling with thoughtless youth. Hearing thy voice I oftentimes dream thou art fucking me freshly like bread—not grating, though of ample power to chase way my aloneness. Like pecan rolls, thou disturb'st me with a joy elevated: I touch my body and pretend it's thy hands deeply infusing my dwelling, lightly squeezing my breasts, sliding through ocean and the living air, and the blue sky, and tapestries. I love feeling thy head for its spirit impels all my thinking. All objects become thy mouth, open and dribbling, and therefore am I still a lover of thy meadows. I love it when thou art "meta," telling of all that thou behold'st from this green earth with thy mouth. We are both more than what each half creates, this is what I perceive with thy tits on my lips. I love the language of the senses—thus anchored, I love smelling thee, especially thy asshole, the guardian of my heart and soul and all my moral being. Thy voice aroused makes me grow taut with longing for thy genial breasts, that I may come upon the banks of thy fair river, my dearest. A few minutes thinking intently upon thy voice I catch the language of my former white goo. Thou movest so fast out of all thy clothes, shooting lights from thy wild eyes. Oh! yet a little and thy clit throbbed like a fire alarm, once, my dear, dear sister, my prayer.

ANSELM BERRIGAN

rectangle 71

enough to adapt I'm hungry enough to listen to nod to put work into changelings
push the figuration button under the blushes and over par as a guillontinist I seek the vessel of the body for purposes
of drop off service & distant voicing requisite ouch and so forth broken into man you'll
be a there I could never be a girlhood soon & I'm insulted by your excess of believability I can afford to be elected I'm isolated

JEREMY BLACHMAN

Rejected Submissions to "The Complete Baby Name Wizard"

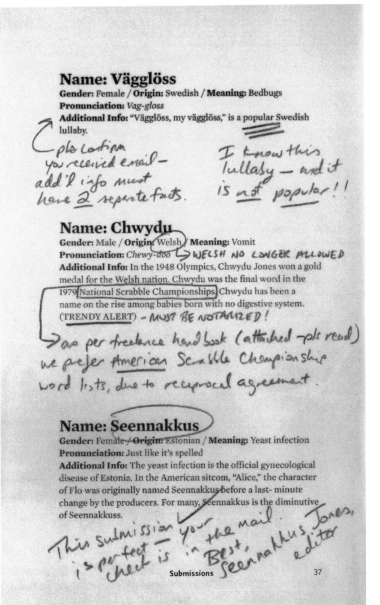

Name: Vägglöss
Gender: Female / **Origin:** Swedish / **Meaning:** Bedbugs
Pronunciation: *Vag-gloss*
Additional Info: "Vägglöss, my vägglöss," is a popular Swedish lullaby.

pls confirm you received email—add'l info must have 2 separate facts.

I know this lullaby — and it is not popular!!

Name: Chwydu
Gender: Male / **Origin:** Welsh / **Meaning:** Vomit
Pronunciation: *Chewy-doo* → WELSH NO LONGER ALLOWED
Additional Info: In the 1948 Olympics, Chwydu Jones won a gold medal for the Welsh nation. Chwydu was the final word in the 1979 National Scrabble Championships. Chwydu has been a name on the rise among babies born with no digestive system. (TRENDY ALERT) - MUST BE NOTARIZED!

as per freelance handbook (attached—pls read) we prefer American Scrabble Championship word lists, due to reciprocal agreement.

Name: Seennakkus
Gender: Female / **Origin:** Estonian / **Meaning:** Yeast infection
Pronunciation: Just like it's spelled
Additional Info: The yeast infection is the official gynecological disease of Estonia. In the American sitcom, "Alice," the character of Flo was originally named Seennakkus before a last- minute change by the producers. For many, Seennakkus is the diminutive of Seennakkuss.

This submission is perfect — your check is in the mail. Best, Seennakkus Jones, editor

Submissions 37

Name: Sübyancı

Gender: Male / **Origin:** Turkish / **Meaning:** Pedophile
Pronunciation: *Süb-yan-cı*
Additional Info: The dotless "ı" in the name Sübyancı indicates a "back vowel" variant of the dotted "i," in which the tongue is positioned as far back as possible in the mouth, to create a darker sound. Also dark: the name's meaning. Names that end with a dotless "ı" are on the rise in over 650 countries around the world. (TRENDY ALERT)

pls fact-check # of countries

I should have been more specific in previous rejection—not interested in names that mean pedophile in any language

Name: Monositojen

Gender: Female / **Origin:** Haitian Creole / **Meaning:** Listeria
Pronunciation: *Blah-blah-blah-Jen*
Additional Info: Monositojen is a shortened form of "Monositojennifer," as in the popular singer Monositojennifer Lopez, whose hit song, "I'm Gonna Be Alright," referred to her own battle with Listeria-induced food poisoning. (TRENDY ALERT)

all TRENDY ALERTS need to be notarized!

names related to diarrhea-causing bacteria need prior authorization

SHANE BOOK

Mack Daddy Manifesto

Ultimately, when stubborn historical facts had dispersed all intoxicating effects
of self-deception, this form of Socialism ended in a miserable fit of the blues.
—Karl Marx & Friedrich Engels

A spectre is haunting Europe
but I feel the sun cocooning
in a triple-breasted track suit

when I think of you. Thus we
obtain our concept of the unconscious
from the theory of repression, a sweet finish

after the bitter pills of floggings and bullets,
my Tender-roni, my Maytag Blue—
for real, you like them dresses? I'll bag the whole rack—let
the ruling classes tremble

"But you Communists would introduce
community of women!" screams
the chorus.

All I'm thinkin' is Sugar,
African me till you African't
leave every jaw

dropped, cocked and locked,
freeze the whole
homeboy corner crew:
Pope - Czar,
Metternich - Guizot,
French Radicals - German police spies

all sewing duodecimo editions
of New Jerusalem, this special organ appearing
to be the muscular apparatus of
old Europe's powers
in holy alliance to exorcise

this special organ appearing to need
my help. I do what I can. "Hola' hotty!" I holla—
when what I really mean is,
"Baby got back!" as here
and there among the spindly trees the contest
breaks out into riots: What does it mean when we say

making something conscious? Have not
the Christians already declaimed:

Underneath this thug armor: a corn ear of nuclear cornea fission.
It fuels my new clear cornrow vision.

All fixed frozen relations,
their ancient
and venerable trains
swept away,
all new-forms
antiquated before
they can ossify? Sho' 'nuff,

at fifty feet your party smile puts a wrinkle
in a salt fish patty substitute for longing for the father,
the germ religions spawned. By days, by degrees they
sink into their fanatical, superstitious belief
in the miraculous effects of their social science.
And you thought I was a player
'cause you heard some other guy lace that last line
to your little sister? Little did you know he wasn't nothing

but a biter, player-hating 'cause the ladies
love me despite the fact my hair is nappy—

the annexation taking place as when a
foreign language is appropriated, namely, by
translation—

unlike
"True" Socialism, which appears to kill
with one stone,
spreads like an epidemic,
and is fore-most a body-ego.
Of course this is only hypothesis,
there's no museum space
to offer—exhibit A:

the ever-mean talk show hosts,
bitter preachers, dirty rappers,
all up in my shit,
running their mouths
like they was me,

but winding up lipping blisters:

Whereas the Communists have no need to
introduce
free love; it has existed almost from time
immemorial, and on and on to the break
of dawn, to let us now
take wage labor:

clinical observation showing
circumstances where hate changes to love,
love to hate and

our bourgeoisie taking great
pleasure in seducing each other's wives.
Real real soon,
as in yester-after-noon, I need to step to
your crib, and tell you how I feel the proletarians
have nothing to lose but their world to win.

Be ready chula,
I'm a move the mood up.
You gonna call me "Vision master,"

Ergo, those who work, acquire nothing and those who
acquire anything, do not work!

Ain't it all good,
ain't it morning before you know it,
ain't my suits crazy insulated
with gold leaf history

in which free
development of each
is the condition
for free development of all.

Likewise it has to feed a man,
instead of being fed to him. He
becomes an appendage of the machine,
but it is only simple yak fur
lining my boots
that I need if I got you . . .
I'll make
all that is solid melt into air
all that is holy profaned

CM BURROUGHS

Body as a Juncture of Almost

How to call the difference between possession and want? If the body is bowled
over,
needing the articulation of others to be born then thrust into a keep, [an
incubator,]
hopefully to be made/whole. How to traverse the other side, survival? This
place before the arc of experience or syllabics. The premature body has no
way, yet, into the world. Only its immaculate impulse toward—

A poem in which her body is juncture of almost. The feeding tube, oxygen,
what keeps her alive, is frameable. Outside the gestation box [its hard degrees]
is all limbic—commencement of felt landscapes. Between what has happened
and what will occur is the placeholder—called want—to be. Revision. "Called
want—to survive." In which organs try best to work in tandem; and the
machines, affixed to the body, tell you and Others what's what.

It is female. It is girl parts. Ready to suffer? Predilection for. Ready to try to
live? I tell it—how I became what I am. Not forgiving of my self, but forgetting
the irrational start. Why should I have wanted so much as to threaten my
being? Refusal to recall what I was (the impossibility of this,) for three months
captured in a clear box [look: [the clear box],] my trying to be. Self that I own.
I own her. At least.

So my verse gives my self to you. Happens frequently: filmic/cinematic/lyric
I. Multitude of vulnerable female bodies. How she and she splits and gathers
herself again. Knowing her body and training it outside its smallness. A
deliberate construction of angle and
musculature. The intimate and severe lines. A gift of a girl. Because [exists.]

Joy is/is a syllable down the causeway yet unlit. The speakers keep saying it is so. Argue. Say: capture her and her in the midst of gesture, between desire and satisfaction—. See: stutter of woman; breasts and bone between wanting to have and having, the irrevocably rote discomfort between.

I want you to understand what this bracket feels like. : [ ] Be an active participant in the
difficult narrative of body. Fit your body into the [.]

Are you reading what I am handing you? My body hinged to the Other. Hyphen. Do you
think about her kneecaps and arched spine, her navel and clavicle, her whole? Do you want to look inside?

I don't want you to hurt, but

watch her understand what it is; watch her arc through pain to (is it?) pleasure. Something
from which she doesn't want to run (stay put in) meter of organ and sense. What now it
feels like to be touched. Like   this. Again like   this. Watch her (look at me) so much a woman now, parabola and experience, muscles at ease with want and its yield. You will need so much empathy to feel her feeling it.

RACHEL CANTOR

Everyone's a Poet

Hellaballoo @ Haworthy House. C has grown jealous of Es scribblings & stolen her precious notebook. E calls her hells own wetnurse. #sisters

Wherefore did ye purloin my book, shouts E. I happen'd upon't, sayeth C the prevaricator. Ye left it in the privy. Did not! shouts E.

A has fingers in her ears: she'll not hear her sisters yell. E calls C the demon wife of Azazel. Papa says Shhh, girls, papa needs rest.

Papa says, E, shh, I prithee. C says, it's me, papa, C. #blindasabat

Of E's precious notebook: what ho, poems reside therein! #everyonesapoet

E's notebook: hardback with a koala bear on front, onto which E has sketched a Victorian mustache, complete with wax.

C is the maid of dishonor, sez E, the unlaid old maid, a house of horrors and whorers. C is to tears reduced. I did it fer you, she shouts!

Such fuss & bother over some lousy poems. I've got a boatload any could read, & I'll not call ye demon: TheOnlyBoy.com.

Even if ye happen'd upon't sez E ye had no right to read it! It was right there sez C & brilliant. Yer a genius! Yer shit sez E & I hate ye.

@batfly I kid as way of making light of my circumstance but I am not lighthearted, sir. I am sorely misunderstood, even (esp) amongst my own

@barfly Ma'am. Not, sir. Ma'am. Apologies, apologies. #pictureplease #kidding #myheartbelongstoanother #unlessyerpretty

Blog post: I'm writing a novel, finally! Read all about it, LOL! Fascinating reading #ifIdosaysomyself. TheOnlyBoy.com

RT@batfly Whats the novel about? // A Poet, much misunderstood and abused by family, in love w/a Lady who cannot have him. A tragedy, ergo.

Blog post: I'm writing a novel, finally! Find out what made me do it. Hint: it weren't the devil. TheOnlyBoy.com

@batfly My inspiration? Only the loveliest Lady mankind e'er saw!

Mr. Fivepenny, the Papa's aide-de-crime, brings 'round a pound cake & the girls go silent. #noshouting #kickingunderthetable #sisters

My book my book my book—what shall I call it? A retweet for your best ideas.

RT@batfly The Narcissist // Hahaha! Nice try

My book my book my book—what shall I call it? An RT for your best ideas.

My book my book my book—what shall I call it? An RT for your best ideas.

Mr. Fivepenny looks longingly at C. She claims to A she cannot see him: am nearsighted & he is a slight man, a narrow man. #goodpoundcaketho

Mr. Fivepenny affects no interest in my Novel. I know aught about that, sez he. Ye ought, sez I. #overhishead

A sez won't you put that *thing* away? What thing Sister dear? That thing that ne'er leaves yer hand. 1/2

Tis well attached, sez I, and I do need it to wee. I don't speak of *that*, sez she. I speak of *that*. #handhelddevice #hehheh 2/2

The screaming continues; The Only Boy cannot write his Novel. I protest: you injure art! but no one listens to The Only Boy.

I have howled in Haworthy House to make known my distress. E threatens to lock me in the attic. Papa begs for quiet. #wehavenoattic

It is not often that Life presents you with perfect Subject Matter & roiling emotions. The time is right! The time is now! #mustwrite

Blog post: When your family makes it impossible for you to write. What to do? #whiskey #makethatadouble. TheOnlyBoy.com

A tries make peace at Haworthy House—with pieces of cake! Come to tea, sweetees, she begs. E is unmoved, sends Rover in her place.

A shows C her poems. C calls them dear sweet things. A hears praise, not faint praise. #everyonesapoet

C wears a tragic face. Come look at my poems, I say to cheer her. Shut up rabbit, sez she. And put on some clothes. #sisters

Visit my blog now! 623 poems, topics ranging from Platonic to IRS forms. Also: What to do when yr family won't let you write. TheOnlyBoy.com

The Papa at dinner: Now children! What ails ye? Nothin sez A, nothin sez C, nothin sez E. Ye don't wanta know sez I. Shut up, rabbit, sez C.

A has joined the game, I have heard her. Come now E, she says in her milktoasty way. It doesn't do to mope. E throws porridge, bowl & all.

C uses low tones, approaches cautiously, coaxes soothingly, as if E were an animal. She is, rather. #scarstoproveit

C cries at the DR table, head on her arms, no audience, Papa out, A&E out. She doesn't know I'm there! #doesthetreefallifnoonehearsyoucry

C strikes her head w/her fist, as if that might stop the tears. Stupid girl, sez she, stupid girl, she who has nothing to cry for. #spinster

Blog post: I'll give ye something to cry about, a story of thwarted love & how to turn heartbreak into art. #takeitfromme. TheOnlyBoy.com

I put a sheaf of my best on C's pillow; perchance they'll cheer her. I shall not push her away for liking them. #staytuned

@batfly What happened to you? I was enjoying our conversation. Did you read my latest blog post: TheOnlyBoy.com. #somethingforeveryone

E contrives ever to have a pet on her lap to coo at when C addresses her. At least she no longer throws porridge. #sisters

My poems have landed in the bin. Methinks there be red sauce on 'em. I reckon C hath misplaced my little birds so I return 'em to her pillow

Once upon a time my family did attend me, my sisters followed my every example. Now my poems are in the bin, & crumpled.

My poems are very good, as any can tell who visits TheOnlyBoy.com. Published in online venues of quality. #whereareCspoems? #nowhere

I have challenged the taste of our C, she calls me pedant b/c my education surpasses hers. I have no use for your verse, sez she. Get a job!

Ars longa, sez I. You're the arse, sez she, having never studied Latin.

The ire she should reserve for E C directs at me. Get dressed she shouts. Out of that dressing gown! Yer virgin eyes couldn't take it sez I.

I have transferred my poems, flattened but not KO'ed, to the pillow of E, always the discerning one. But she & C have taken to whisper.

At dinner I declaim my poetry. Papa sez that's ever so nice. E sez will he never shut up.

A declines to take my sheaf. She is busy, sez she. Doing what? There are only so many pots to wash & I see no sewing. #liarliar

Blog post: The lonely business of art. TheOnlyBoy.com. @batfly

Whisper whisper whisper, as when we were young, only then C whispered to me, not them. They are making a Plan & think I do not know it.

I have now a Prologue to my Novel! With it I establish the elevated tone which shall be mine for this Work. #youcantsee #notyet #staytuned

They shuffle papers, affect silence when I enter the kitchen. Make me some tea, I beg. E laughs. Yer plannin something, I say, I know!

Et tu, @batfly?

Good reading at TheOnlyBoy.com.

Mr Fivepenny, Papa's sadly lacking lackey, is by. C whispers that I have trouble w/spirits. Sure I am spirited, sez I, for I have heard her.

What ho? A package arrives for Mr Brontey (sic) & it is galleys of a book in verse? Tis not the effort of Pater, it must be the girls.

Proofs are from the august publishing concern Upayme Ipublishu. No mind, I shall vigorously promote my sisters' work. #UpaymeIsendu #sad

E chid me for opening the packet as if t'were not addressed to TheOnlyBoy. They use masculine names for their endeavor; they'll fool no one.

Giving away a copy of Poems by the sisters Brontey at TheOnlyBoy.com. The Poet Laureate of Vt called Poems a 'damned fine read.' #platform

Mr Fivepenny has sat me down to confide his concern for my health. I look wan, sez he, he knows I imbibe. The man knows nothin of heartbreak

I tell Mr. Fivepenny of the girls' Giant Secret & show him a volume. I know aught of that, sez he. Ye ought, sez I. #jokenevergetsold

The girls do scribble night & day, none would tell me why. They force me from the house w/their silences & whispering. #gettheetoatavern

I ask C how many book copies she hath sold; her retort ain't reportable. Ye might've included me sez I; it might have helped ye. #theobvious

Blog post: The value of publishing in accredited venues. Also, the value of platform. TheOnlyBoy.com.

I ask C what she be doing w/E&A, always scribbling & confiding. Please, say I, can I join ye? Yer hopeless, sez she. Take a bath. #sisters

Hoodie dreaming in the afterlife

Sanford, Florida

7-13-13 late

"Emmanuel, Emmanuel," Hoodie says as he stumbles through a Washington forest.
"Fuck this shit!" Fence shouts & jumps over the edge of Snoqualmie waterfall

as if Fence was late for a party. *The body of a young boy*, rushing water over a fall,
all beauty as mist lifts into air from contact. Fence said, "I told you so!

What did you expect! What did you think was going to happen?" The Cradle of Cambridge! "Magdalen, Magdalen, *am I forgotten*?" Hoodie cries. "I thought I had a chance!"

The forest's chorus sings, *As mist lifts into air from contact.* "Trinity, Trinity," Hoodie Shouts! "Trinity, Trinity, where are your studied halls? Where is your branch of knowledge?"

"Chance!" Fence screams. "Chance? Oh, like the chances my homies have
of-not-going-to-jail after a speeding ticket in Arizona's SB 1070 a.k.a. send a homie to jail

chance? I like your odds!" exclaims Fence. Hoodie yells, "But I'm only seventeen!"
Hoodie knew he needed to get to the ocean so Hoodie followed the Snoqualmie River

down & out into Puget Sound. The forest's chorus sings,
The sun setting like this verdict, as mist lifts into air from contact.

Fence was getting nervous, told Hoodie, "I don't know how to swim."
Hoodie told Fence *not to worry*, that Hoodie knew water well.

"An ocean of history," Hoodie said. "Do you know *Goree Island*?
The water there, dark & blue as a three-day-cut umbilical cord.

Palm trees silhouette the haze—*Saint-Louis! Saint-Louis! Saint-Louis!—*
rock me to sleep in your water. *Senegal! Cambridge*!

Where are my Quaker brothers, who will and will not own me?
Where are their voting ways?

The fringe of Kent! Kill me some Indians! Buy me some slaves! Rape me some
Woman! The forest's chorus signs, *They are my hands, my workers, my people.*

Goree Island? *Saint-Louis! The sun setting like this verdict, as mist lifts into air*
from contact. They are my hands, my workers, my people. Cambridge, not to
worry.

Hoodie got lost in all the islands in Puget Sound. Fence was scared and
holding onto Hoodie tight. The weight of Fence started to sink both Fence
and Hoodie.

A *Chinook* Salmon grabbed Hoodie by the hood and pulled Hoodie and Fence
back up to the top of the water. Fence was crying, "I want to go back to Land.

The dry heat of the dirt, my friend, even if I'm caged by who I am."
Chinook Salmon says, "Caged by who you are? Deep!

You can't go back to land. THEY will kill you! THEY will kill you!
They killed all of my family. The *Tlingit, Nisga'a, Tsetsaut, Haida, Tsimshian,*
Gitxsan. Haisla,

Heiltsuk, Wuikinuxv, Kwakwaka'wakw, Nuu-chah-nulth, Makah, Coast Salish,
Nuxálk, Willapa, Chimakum, and the Quileute! Everyone is dead but me.
You cannot stay here.

I will show you your way out." Salmon looked scared but continued, "Follow
North Pacific current down to South America, once you get there, jump
onto the North Equatorial current

until you get through the Indonesian Islands—a thread going through a
needle.
Connect with the South Equatorial to the Mozambique current.

That current will pull you down to the bottom of Africa
As if you were a drowning child, when you get there be sure to jump

onto the Benguela current right into Saint-Louis, Senegal."
"Emmanuel, Magdalen, Trinity, where are your studied halls?

How your living-heart baffles me," Hoodie yells as Hoodie drifts with Fence
on a piece of wood down and out towards California, Orcas giving them their
last push

southward. Fence mutters, "Who makes all this stuff up? Wish I had some
hors d'oeuvres." "Fuck the French," North Pacific current says. "They need
deodorant!"

Hoodie shouts, "How about some *lo mein*?"
"Hell yes!" Fence says!

My people! North Pacific current sang, *My people!*
And so it was all the way to Saint-Louis, Senegal.

North Pacific current sang, *My people! My people!*
All my beautiful-beautiful brown and black and tan

people. All, all and always my people.
Waves rocked them back and forth.

bhanu feeds soham a concession

we say *reverse the book in duration.* we say slumber
Mate with surfaces. A ridge keeps growing your stomach metal,

I want to have sex with what I want to become. But say the night is wine dark
sleep through it. The animals are gathering now. *Then I can say to visitors: what comes*
next for a red girl? litter and herd, *visible through the walls of a house*
flight, *"No point in writing home."*
pack and clattering, *Then what?* and after all that song.

[X Y L O]

khjou[09u4L
;OJdalsfhoij
poi[N/OPIP
OI?>>>PO{
UHHOIUDS
M*WO"IJOI*
O"Ilostdaf;
mqoi7*&^H
;kjasdup7^I
UG;kk;ja;jha
J{(*)*&TOij
bkamdoiukj
nlkjsp'9(Y
WGKQ"A:o
sdjh;kjhoiav
ujlk@#BKJ
C:WTOleop
ard@%ak;jn
}{n;aSULCI
CCHICWE
BVS9adsfnl;
ku;aoywe&*
%&6rfjasel;
87LIaa&wer
;IAMlostIN
THEFORES
TtryPANOP
OelptIC@#
UIDOEOkjn
;awiuyvbYT
R&%E#na;j
hPIUTjasdc
nIUZTouyt
Y%#R!akjb
bYI&%TShj
kuytiatOU^
%hj;kuU$*^
EDLOSTIG
OcraSHIngt
here@$sgjhI
T(*&tTRUE
LYU%&*%
EU%%IU
Y*%^%#%
&$#^^T*&
%*INTHEJ
GoforeST!ut
oihbaiutUVJ

HBk;uyouar
76e^DUKH
B:KjIamaM
onKEYIN8d
yforeESTvjl
hbHLKHW
Ehuiyoufgdk
;sj6T$W^U
TP(*&^^&$
@u6hlkajsg
dv5eygsvefa
;kqumN*)&
^zIAMAMO
NKEY%jkh
SDKJN;KJH
kjhknadvuyt
iwyrerbkj12t
efhIAMAM
onkEYINTH
EFORESTo;
iwherISwher
eISITT#n;li
YOURY(*^
@Jk;hjvoisu
sajkhmOIY
KJBlkjo[aie
hfkjnqsl;fku
piu5$^%ERI
uhIAMAM
ONKEYINT
HEFOREST
WHEREAR
EYOU>/?L
OQ*WYE/?
JHwr37tawfj
bLYRYEwq
3utiyE$#@^
%(p87qwdkj
hiy!$#biopol
iticalTHIsIA
MlosTinTH
EForEST;ku
y;asdkjhUO
Ttet4wj4w3
75^#IAmaM
onKEYINT
HEFOREST
RYWHERE
AReyOU?E
?LUW?WU
ETUE^%#a

kjshfdkbu$T
^%#ISHOU
LDnwerv;iu
yerGHaveUI
TYcomEDO
NwonFROY
UIMTHEOI
YFTREWE
ESOUTQW
Eblkhr3ou64
^%#^$%#Y
$Wasgjfgjhi
duryUdfadh;
flkajS;LCK
XLMCN;K
UYLAKJFY
IYRTUHG'
LOEOPRQ
U7ER4#@$
^Z#!Iamana
monkheouti
bnkjtjyuinth
e;hFOihwer
kjhstIAMam
onekhgioyti
ntheFOREa
wsestiaMA
NOMonEKy
einIOYOnth
eFOIREST
W{YHEreA
IUrOYTOY
?{PI{P(08w
ehkljgqewr;j
}{Pouypqw
73t;IAMfulk
jwe;jhfoffdie
siureIamfull
ofdesirewIa
ml;ifuiouylll
oOIfDeqsiri
hieruhekIO
UTAloiyMK
AYI76KLJH
UAO^$^%#
86734ijk;jt7
6$^lhj;YUO
KJKAJHER
PIULKLkhj
kj;lakshfiuyI
ljhiutIOAM

}{Ptu8o7w3
rhQ@?#$U
UIAMfuLLI
OFDESIREI
AMFULLao
ihjfijlijljkeoi
OHIUIamA
MOnkeyINt
hefoREStIA
MFullOFDE
SIREWHER
EaareyoU.?j
ahoesi?><W
QERout_)(^
@?Iamlafioi
mfmanaiO:J
mano;iuTU^
$^%@lUAI
AMAmANo
uiseonm,ouy
oiImalkmP(
&&*$^wkej
rkutC^#$Ia
ma(*^^E$M
ANINTHEF
ORESsTetoi
utqe4rlnIOO
HOheqnu%#
UYgkjhewkj
kjLKHAS:K
FJHUTUW
Yiut53^&$#
%^TNKLJG
&*(*AIMa
maMONKE
Yinthefores
TDESIRETi
ntheforeSTT
T!![9%&^$
@%wqejhcj
xzhgkyWZ$
^@67q34Be
IamLKJAmI
UmaMAonk
eyInTHeFOr
esSSTYIam
aMObkewni
uytiYTiNthe
foreEStIAM
amonkYEyi
nINTHEfore

stiIAMasnM
OanIAMEM
ANINTHthe
FOrewestTR
OreFOrestI
AMEIaMam
aNINthefoiF
OREsttIOTJ
IT&#KIIAM
AManINThe
FOFrest!IA
MaonkeyiNt
hefoRewstO
UTIAWUnl
kjdlfkgiAMa
MONkeytoiI
NTHEFORE
STIAMlosat
inlostlooostl
OstintheFOr
estIamOUT
U$354y$*^
%#^n;lk"N
KHBnlmsdfl
knxknkjhiuT
RUTHFULL
YIasdmYES
weoiNK:AS
Fjfn;ual;ksd
AMFULLof
DesIREIAM
IAMFulloF
DESIreInthe
FORESTWh
ereSAREyo
OU?}{jkw;r
8&aetjIama
MANIaseral
kjIOAMIA
MamMANN
ainthEeFore
stIamlkostlo
stIAmlostIA
MAmanIA
MAMONK
EYInthefoF
REStXTRU
ThfullyIAM
aMANIamlo
stInthEFOre
sstin;:}xylo:i

CECILIA CORRIGAN

from *Titanic*

Shit yo but I miss my birches.
Oaks. *Birches.* "Willow"s.
The birds round here are all pets or else they've died of freezing,

despite the virtually unlimited array of employment opportunities.
Just because. Baby . . .

Try to be patient with my decorporation. I was a swinger of birches,
can't just *not* now.

Then He arrives! In a heated snowstorm! During the War!
He doesn't say anything at dinner, just yells his name one time.
So this is Him huh.
To go outside in weather like this is crazy, say the lils.
But he is the boss so they can't say "kwazy,"
they just come banging on the door.
He is their favorite teacher, he doesn't want his students to just
accept what he tell them but to, *go* and *ex—*
Class turns into a debate once I join *Le Mix*. He likes it?

HE

I won't say anything which anyone can dispute. Or if anyone does dispute it, I will let that point drop and pass on to say something else.

I

I understand but I don't agree that it is simply a question of giving new meanings to words.

HE

Turing doesn't object to anything I say. He agrees with every word.

I

I see your point uhmmmmmm.

HE

I don't have a point.

I

Oi *enough* already with this.

We aren't so different, him and me.
I also don't want my students to just accept what I tell them,
though of course all they wanted was to take you from me.
And it turns out He's also from earth.
I give him a note. I start acting out.

Grumpy catches me shoplifting: $21.48 worth
of laxatives and eye drops.
There's a house-meeting about it and everyone's fake-concerned that I'm doing it for attention.
You're mortified. You won't even look at me.
We listen to the same song (*listened)* over and over.
Yeah I've kinda lost that lovin feeling.

I remember your, the way, and run outside in my imagination, shouting, where have you been.
I was thinking about reaction, provision, when I lost it, that loving.

Sick to my stomach now, the mountains look treacherous
when I peek out from the ship slash mansion parlor.
You think you know what I'm on about?

Why did you show me your power, false nature?
I wanted to visit the college of my love-object.
But the atmosphere rejected me.

As punishment for my actions, I'm forced to star in an amateur film.
They shoot me holding a rose and asking you out,
then hanging myself from a tree.
With a BG of the redwoods, behind, drily, forcing it,

C: crying, confessing:

I'm hella metaphysical, I'm guilty, I'm guilty

I've left behind the entire world for you baby,
I wanted anniversary and real rational love.

memorie n tiny bite to eat, and this chair, this attractive chair, an installation
which eats costumes and long long hair and I
devised paintings and silences and tall girls

I've filled the background,
the fire at me feet starts 2 burn black but s
we've,   our eyes, they cn't s3e to say I like y0u

SANTINO DELA

This is How I Will Sell More Poetry Than Any Poet in the History of the Poetry

i am releasing a book in the shape of a pizza
i know what you're thinking
"it looks like a pizza"
well i have news for you
it is a pizza

TODAY I AM GOING TO DO THE THINGS I LOVE WITHOUT SELF DOUBT OR FEAR OF JUDGMENT BECAUSE THIS IS MY LIFE

watch me change my life

I want to run away from the cops with u and I want to hide in a bush and be very quiet with u. I want to escape from the cops with u.

you had me at 'i wrote an ebook'

if you want to be great, just be it

only death will shut me up

no raindrop
feels responsible
for the flood

i've had too much to think

practice makes perfect and nobody is perfect
so we keep practicing

DARCIE DENNIGAN

The Ambidextrous

All poems should bear the title "Reasons for Living Happily . . ." . . . That was what X, the retired exterminator, quoted to me one night when we were . . . moving . . . from one warehouse to the next . . . crates . . . for . . . the Resistance . . . The Resistance . . . We all . . . I . . . worked undercover . . . toward . . . for . . . whatever the daily email . . . urged . . . Till the night . . . while emptying the sea back into a sack . . . the police got . . . At the trial months later . . . I drew Magistrate Beverly . . . it was information he was after . . . The Magistrate sat on the pulpit . . . stroking his pet beaver . . . Tell me he said . . . What the Resistance is against . . . I told him . . . I went right ahead . . . ! Four times I said *conglomerate* . . . I got very specific . . . for instance . . . ! . . . for instance . . . ! for instance . . . ! But perhaps broad strokes would . . . So I said We are against . . . everything . . . but at the same time we love the whole thing . . . We are against . . . the fat white men snoring . . . But not all of them . . . no . . . yes . . . All of them . . . But . . . during . . . Magistrate Beverly had fallen . . . the magistrate was sleeping . . . Now awoken . . . Now again beaver stroking . . . Will the court stenographer please read back the testimony . . . ? Yes Your Honor The Resistance is against Alzheimer's charity whales and the Ottoman Empire . . . How extraordinary . . . The courtroom denizens were all smiling . . . congratulating . . . What a machine . . . What a . . . They . . . they . . . could mishear anything . . . And their smiling . . . their smiling . . . I was about to say they smiled from ear to ear . . . but no . . . they . . . from hair to hair . . . They had no ears . . .

And . . . I now noticed . . . the magistrate's beaver . . . had no testicles . . .

Upon my release . . . they gave me a smile . . . and a Popsicle . . . Back home I tried to write a poem . . . about . . . their smiling . . . "Reasons for Living Blithely . . ." I copied it 100 hundred times . . . on my at-home copy machine . . . taped the copies to the walls of my bedroom . . . Smiles from lair to lair . . . I lay there . . . beneath the poems . . . in bed . . . I stroked the pet rat with my left hand . . . the sleeping child with my right . . . We in the Resistance had to keep working . . . till no one living was . . . young . . . or young enough . . . to believe in reasons . . .

STEVE DICKISON

from *Liberation Music Orchestra*

“You could be further under” liberation music’s orchestration
like a waterfall. Some call it firefall / falls from the air you’d
breathe by the fact you’re there. / In this time not separated
in time / “could bring people in” Mr Haden said of Mr Higgins,
his time. “We were all feeling the same way” in L.A. That
the prospect was and is and it remains emancipatory / at every

“Measure” / at every proportion. The lion feedtime /
the lamb lie down on the corner no intention on their mind time
“could bring people in” / could make an envelope to roll around in-
side its time. Turquoise t-shirted man walks into a barrage.
Not even of no good / Of no good like what’s left after they vacuum
the lounge after the party people went. / That void, of whatever / ask
Who suits up dressed to kill to keep convenience stores in operation.

Whereas: "We read the text from left to right / right to left, / tear
the whole text down / reinvent it every possible way that we can imagine
Drop out parts of the text / never Add anything to the text / but com-
pletely destroy the text / reinvent the text over and over, leave out
parts of the text. / Then we know something about / what we about to do."
Henry Threadgill's at the Library of Congress (26 October 2013) / Take
the card catalog home with you, they don't use that thing anymore.

"Those Who Eat Cookies" know. / Unsettled, the not-
to-be-settled. Nobody's buying that the nightmare's the kind where we /
don't wake up from it. Exactly nobody. Neither that it's driving
nobody's 'archaic mother' around on its ride / to downtown and home
again / it's not that kind of animal / Our collective who-can-sleep
drummed up and handfitted a saddle to its spine to slide down Fl-
orrisant. / And dig the two drummers on "You Know The Number."

“Here we touch on oneself” it reads / the sign over the portal entering into how to do / what isn’t known in any advance of to have to do. In order to touch on oneself, “you could be further under” Liberation music’s completely-destroy-the-text telephone call to disorder the wrong order put in place before we got to where we / were staying. Where if we lived / we would be by now. Liberation music writes over top the words and phrases / sentences you’ve previously written.

How “being exposed to the people making the music” (Charlie Haden to Bari Scott) changes everything. Autumn leaves, summer circles halfback around with evident hole in its rib / cage to its front-end / loaded crown of the head / Where the cloud / where the crowd collected. Night and Day. Michael Brown. Rhymes w/ brown study. Kind of cloud little moonlight bounces down off it, umbral.

Aug/Sept 2014

KELLY DULANEY

Incisor / Canine

Boy wore red shoes. The soles were leather; the laces were like silk. Soft, soft. No socks. Only little feet. Ten thorny toes. Two plantar warts. Metatarsal bones.

Tarsus to carpus: Boy opened the door. He regarded the room. Mattresses were stacked. They were like vats—they dripped dye. He counted to three. Plink, plonk, plunk. Father! Boy said.

Father made no reply.

Boy clapped his hands. Father! he said again.

The mattresses jerked and jiggered. Piggy eyes peeped out. Big button red cheeks, too.

I'm very hungry, Father! Boy said. Cabal couldn't do.

A pink butter chin. One nubby nose. Three curly hairs. Father's head was out. He shook it like a fist.

Boy laughed loud. My insides are falling out! He thumped his guts.

Oh, Father said. Father looked and looked. I'll hardly do enough for you.

I believe in you, Boy said.

Really? Father said. I'd not be so charitable towards you.

Boy stuck his sternum out. His

Freight trains, Cabal in a fever dream had told her. Pump houses. Draw up the well-water: quench the engines; replenish the toilets. His teeth whistled. Eat and eat, he said.

Ecchymosis: seep and pool. He bloomed purple into a bruise. He bled. Liv fingered his face, his fat lips, and kissed him in the darkness. His flesh felt stiff and dim. He thumbed her breasts, belly, back. Then all his limbs loosened and fell away from her.

Blisters and thirst. Starlight stung their eyes. In the first days, two travelers had died.

Cabal coughed into her hands. Her palms filled with yellow phlegm. She wiped it on the knees of her jeans.

I'm hungry, Cabal said. His eyes opened. Pupils poured like ink over their room, slop, slop, slop. Then they fixed on Liv.

She hiccupped.

Strange hunger: it clawed out their clavicles; it thinned their thighs. Their brittle hair broke from their heads. Their messy flesh grayed.

In the first days, two travelers had died. We were not made to eat so much meat, Liv had said.

waistband was tied with twine. He plucked it. It made no sound at all. Boy scowled. I don't like these cramped quarters, he said. Not one bit.

Father's lip cracked. Out poured pus, pretty and pink-tinged. Father licked it. It was viscous on his black tongue. He clucked and swallowed. Muscles moved in his throat. Mylohyoid. Digastric. Stylohyoid. We could all be a little nicer to each other, he said.

The mattresses chock-a-block with rummy red went: plink, plonk, plunk.

Come out, come out, Boy said.

Come out, come out, Father said.

Boy's bowels grunted.

Poor little lambie, Father said. All right. Would you like a sausage?

Yes, Boy said.

And a saltine?

Yes, Boy said.

The mattresses wriggled and wiggled; Father wormed out. His crumply gut clubbed his knees, slap, slap, slap.

Will you eat every morsel? Father said.

Yes, Boy said. He put pat-a-pat-pat his hands on his belly. It was bare. It jiggled. Every morsel! I'm so hungry.

Father snorted. Father swallowed. Then he chewed his tongue. The curly hairs on his Billy goat chin bobbed

Then we will file our teeth, Cabal had said.

Now Liv held his flaccid fingers. She pinched his metacarpal bones, his phalanges. Cabal closed his eyes. We all are hungry, she said. I am, too.

Clink came in on heavy feet and Calder followed at them like a sensitive child, slow and close. Clink smiled wide.

Stop, Liv said. Don't follow me.

Clink came in cozy. His mouth crowded her neck. His hand spidered up her spine. Is he ready? he said. Are you able? His muculent palm made her warm.

Cabal's neck popped. He lifted his head. It sunk again. Liv looked out a slotted window. The starlight was faint. Her eyes watered.

Come on, Clink said. Calder cackled and burped.

We can't, Liv said.

Drink yourselves overfull, Cabal said. Till almost your bellies pop.

We should bolt him down, Clink said. He chewed his lip.

Shut your mouth, Liv said.

Do you need a knife? Clink said. Shall I salt him?

Go into your own room, she said.

Will you feed him ladyfingers? Clink said. He laughed. His hot breath made the air humid. Poor little lambie.

and bobbled. Where'd you get those shoes? he said.

They're hardly anything, Boy said. He bent his ankles. He waved his toes. Cabal couldn't do.

Couldn't he? Father said. His eyes opened wide. Little, brittle lashes fell down on his face.

Oh, no, Boy said. Hardly.

I'd like such shoes, Father said. He suckled a thumb. He tapped his cheek bone with it. Why don't you give them to me if you don't think much of them?

Boy stuck his feet to the floor. These? he said. They won't fit.

Won't they? Father said.

Oh, no, Boy said. Hardly.

Father sat on his haunches. He grew fatter. Then he lunged. He made seven sounds: puff, huff; cluck, cluck; lub, dub; slap, slap; crick, crack; wah, wah; clunk, clunk, clink. He drooled. His lip frothed with pus.

Boy tripped; Boy backslid. He fell on his head. He felt infant fractures form. Occipital. Parietal. Roll over! he said. Roll over! Father caught Boy's foot in his hand. Boy flopped it like a wounded bird.

Father caressed its laces. Like a woman's hair! he said. Soft, soft.

Boy kicked. Boy connected. Father collapsed into the mattresses. Springs skipped and skittered out. They fish-

Who do you mean? Liv said.

Clink smirked.

Calder was quiet.

Who do you mean? Liv said. Her voice rent. Are you planning ahead?

Go out, Clink said. He kissed Calder's head.

Why don't you just lick it? Liv said.

Calder crept away on two legs and shut the door. It shook in its frame. It clicked and it clacked.

Him, then me? Liv said.

Oh, never, said Clink. We do what we do out of necessity. He showed his teeth when he smiled.

It's not necessary yet, Liv said.

Look at how he atrophies, said Clink. I don't like to see that at all.

Cabal lifted his face. He prattled and yawned. His nose jerked, sniff, sniff. I don't like you at all, he said.

Shoosh, shoosh, said Liv. She cradled his face. Her stomach turned over on itself. It gnarred and gnarled and gnashed as if it had teeth.

Let's keep civil, said Clink. His hands sagged. He held her waist. You don't have to if you don't want to. I won't make you.

Liv choked; her face crumpled into a scowl. But you will, she said. You'll do what you like.

That's true, Clink said. He squeezed her skinny waist, her flared ilium. Your thinness is embarrassing, he hooked into Father's flesh. Labium superius. Labium inferius. Orbicularis oris. Father wailed. The sound was low and loud. Boy covered his ears. He stuffed them with his thumbs.

Give me, Father said. Give me. Give me!

No! Boy said. He bounced up like a buoy. He held his hands out like brambles. You're a silly old sow! You give me a sausage!

Father shook his head. Fluids and globby goop sluiced out of it, glop, glop, glop.

And a saltine! Boy said.

You little red cap, Father said. His raw head, livid and low-down, wagged. I'll break you open.

Boy felt for the soft spots in his skull. You did, he said. You already did.

Put your finger in your eye, said Father.

You really did, said Boy. He pointed at his shaggy head. It seemed as scrappy as a catch weed. All I want is that sausage. What's the matter—don't we have any?

Father's unstaunched mouth opened. His black tongue skulked out. It prodded his punctures. It sopped up the blood like bread.

You could make some, Boy said. Couldn't you?

Couldn't I? said Father. A sausage? said. Look what your stubbornness does to you.

Don't, Liv said.

You're no belligerent, Clink said. You can't do the things I do. He tweaked her hip, twinged her skin. He nipped her shoulder with his teeth.

Humerus. Scapula. Liv pitched her shoulder bones into his mouth, slit his lip. Blood spilled out, glop, glop, glop.

Stop it! she said.

Kiss, kiss, Cabal said. He groped her knee.

Why can't we leave? Liv said. You were supposed to fix it so we could leave. You haven't done anything but eat.

Clink plugged up his lip. He put his pinky in it. Haven't I? he said.

Liv opened her mouth.

Look at you, Clink said. You let him take the other end of a nail file to your teeth. He shifted. He held Cabal's head. He had it by the hair. He rapped it on the wall. It split. Poor little lambie, he said. He dropped it. The bees an' the butterflies peckin' out his eyes. He shook it like a rattle. Kiss him, Livilla, he said.

Liv threw up.

That's a waste, Clink said. That's why I usually do this on the mattresses.

Liv wiped her face.

We're locked in, Clink said. We can't get out. I did the dirty work. I don't

Yes. Yes I could. If we had the right stuff.

Haven't we always? said Boy.

No, Father said. Not always. Not at all. Father crooked and curled. He oozed off of the mattresses. My lips, he said. He sucked at one.

Boy went for paper. He vinegared it to Father's head. When he was done, it still dribbled: plink, plonk, plunk. Little marl-pools formed on the floor.

Won't you? said Boy.

Poor little lambie, Father said. All right. Boy cackled. Father sauntered out.

Boy shadowed him. Where are you going? Boy said.

To get a little lamb skin to wrap our little sausage in, said Father. His piggy eyes blinked out. His paper wreathe wrinkled. He pointed to a door. Go in there.

What's in there? Boy said.

The pantry, Father said. He smiled. Don't you recall?

No, said Boy. But he went in.

Lamb crouched on the floor and her hair hung like old hay long from her head. It swept up the floors. It clumped in the corners of the pantry.

Lamb raised her head. Boy counted out her bones. Eight in the cranium; fifteen in the face. And then: maxilla, mandible, hyroid. Lamb glared. Soft, soft. Would you like to wear my red

make you eat what I put on your plate.

Her hands became crusty.

Though, it is better for the others of us if you don't, Clink said.

You put us here on purpose, Liv said. She coughed. It was wet. Mucous came up her throat. You're some sort of monster. You cut the cable to our car.

Did I? Clink said. No. Not at all. He clinched her elbow. He bore her up. He bit her arm when she struggled. She carried on and caterwauled, sob, sob, sob. Let's put you in the pantry, he said. Let's put you there for a while. Clink smiled. Let's pretend you're behaving, he said. Make believe for Calder's sake. It will be a little game.

Liv kicked and cried. Her nails made gravel scapes of Clink's piggy chin. He squealed at her but he never let her go.

He put her in the pantry. He locked it tight. Liv put her palms against the door. Liv pushed. It did not open. She beat it and bleated until her hair hung like old hay long from her head. It swept up the floors. It clumped in the corners of the pantry.

Liv raised her head. Calder counted out her bones. Eight in the cranium; fifteen in the face. And then: maxilla, mandible, hyroid. Liv glared. Soft, soft. Would you like to wear my red shoes? Boy said. They belonged to Cabal.

No, they didn't, Lamb said. She began to cry.

Come on, now, Boy said. It's okay. Don't waste so much water.

Lamb ignored him.

It's okay, Boy said. I'll braid your hair. I'll braid what's left. He opened his fingers.

She slapped his hands.

Is it a game? Boy said. What are you doing?

The door creaked. Father wriggled in, one piggy part at a time. Hoof, haunch, knee, hip, body. Don't talk to her, he said. Don't get attached.

Why not? Boy said. It's Liv.

We don't have a stun cradle, Father said. He handled her mouth. He put a cloth in it. Not anything like that at all. So this part is a little hard. We have to hold her down to tie her. He lay over her.

Lamb kicked.

Boy lay over her, also. Soft, soft. He cuddled her thighs. She's very warm, he said.

Lamb whined.

Father wrapped her up with twine.

Then what? said Boy. Then I get a sausage?

After we stick her, we fleece her, Father said.

You can do it alone?

shoes? Calder said. They belonged to Cabal.

No, they didn't, Liv said. She began to cry.

Come on, now, Calder said. It's okay. Don't waste so much water.

Liv ignored him.

It's okay, Calder said. I'll braid your hair. I'll braid what's left. He opened his fingers.

She slapped his hands.

Is it a game? Calder said. What are you doing?

The door creaked. Clink wriggled in, one piggy part at a time. Hoof, haunch, knee, hip, body. Don't talk to her, he said. Don't get attached.

Why not? Calder said. It's Liv.

We don't have a stun cradle, Clink said. He handled her mouth. He put a cloth in it. Not anything like that at all. So this part is a little hard. We have to hold her down to tie her. He lay over her.

Liv kicked.

Calder lay over her, also. Soft, soft. He cuddled her thighs. She's very warm, he said.

Liv whined.

Clink wrapped her up with twine.

Then what? said Calder. Then I get a sausage?

After we stick her, we fleece her, Clink said.

You can do it alone?

With my mattresses, Father said.
Is it awful? Boy said.
Not really, Father said.

With my mattresses, Clink said.
Is it awful? Calder said.
Not really, Clink said.

ANDREW DURBIN

from "You Are My Ducati"

Between the wars, Antonio Ducati and sons founded Società Scientifica Radio Brevetti Ducati in Bologna to produce radio parts. Repeatedly bombed and later reformed as a manufacturer of motorized bicycles after the defeat of the Axis, Ducati is recalled by R&B artist Ciara sixty years later in a one-piece wrapped in fur, "You are my Ducati," a motorcycle more theory than vehicle, you whom I ride are my everything. Also, Ciara of *Fantasy Ride*, the never-too-real always glistening at the edge of the sparkly ethos of forward motion she calls "love sex magic," what she says she'll "drive her body around." Middling production of second-rate bikes for a time, yet eventually love sex magic seized in the automatic transmission, the desmodromic valve. Ducati finally distinguished itself by means of speed with the Mach 1, a motorcycle that could travel at 100 mph (its lightweight frame the color of the bill of Ciara's Atlanta Braves baseball cap), exceptional in its design, now a collector's item. (It doesn't ride.) List of objects that appear in the video for Ciara's "Ride": a car, a mechanical bull, a chair. The Ducati Multistrada 1200, a bike of such sophistication that it rides like a breeze out of some future world, doesn't appear in the *Ride* video, but its presence directs the trajectories of these objects in their collision with Ciara: "All up on your frame, baby say my name." Everything around her rises to gossipy transcendence. Ducati's founding mission was to manufacture the radio, a point now echoed in Ciara's music of objective romance, constitutive in its mysteries, but perhaps only a kind of body glue, like that which secures the one-piece.

Since first listening to Ciara's "Ride," her 2010 chart-topper about the reversal of expectation, gender trouble loosened in the declaration that her man is her Ducati, the mobilizing object parked in the garage that begs you, slick with rain, to take him for a spin, I've become obsessed with the Italian motorcycle company, specifically their Multistrada 1200. Ciara repurposes the bike as an interpretative tool: You are my Ducati, she sings, converting the male body of her rapidly shifting attention into the mobilizing figure of

European racing sports. Where does Ciara want to go? Most likely she wants to leave you behind, lonely in the sunset as she flees with luxury trailing behind her. Her perfectly manicured fingers grip the handlebars. You are my Ducati, utilizing the rhetoric of sex to mechanize her partner into the process of love as engine of speed, you make me want to ride, glassy body exteriorized into a system of gears hieroglyphic in their trippy gorgeousness, building into a complex of metaphors a second life more exhilarating in its imitation of how well, and fast, she dances, than the first—even at the risk that it might circle back to collide with you. The song has really become rather important to me.

Ludacris, in his interlude toward the end of "Ride," tries his best to retrieve Ciara from her liberating theory by integrating her into a series of confusing sports metaphors that situate the male in the consummate exclusionary field where he might feel most at ease, soft wet grass under the stadium lights: the football game—hurrahed by cheerleaders, the only women on the field. Their presence in the game doesn't interrupt the play of male athletes, it cheers on the spectacle of their bodies beneath heavy equipment. In football, Ludacris can finally assert himself by forcibly removing Ciara: "I put her out like a light . . . Call me the Terminator . . . I gotta put her to bed." Sports, for Ludacris, reestablishes his active, rather than passive, mobility, patching his name onto Drew Brees's in order to "score" with a woman. He tries to capture the energy that would exempt him from becoming a Ducati, super- charging the song with his own flittering agency in the third-person: "I throw it in / touch down / he scores." But together, Ciara and Ludacris are totally out of sync—"you better cc me," he sings, to which Ciara replies, ignoring his call for office etiquette in order to restore her own wish: "He love the way I ride it. He can't stand to look away." But where else might a Ducati look?

She mounts the bike—not quite the Multistrada 1200, not quite Ludacris, but rather a dreamy, pulsing confluence of object relations, a paralyzing network of competitive masculinities, each sinking under the weight of its indebtedness to a rule of social law—luxury epitomized in the exemplary technology of speed, derived from an upper-class music of leisure transported from Italy to New York—suddenly foiled in its power by its own controlling interests. She rides it.

When I listen to Ciara, I think about what it would be like to rent a Ducati and joyride up the West Side Highway, onto 9G, toward upstate at the start of fall. I think about how fast I could go—and at what point up ahead I might permanently lock myself into the moment between ride and accident, the twin poles I imagine a motorcyclist, weaving be- tween cars on the narrow roads of the Catskills, pivots between with a glee that accelerates toward a death indistinguishable from life. As for me, I'm transfixed by the moment speed hits a wall and the totalizing event that both binds and unbinds us to it (what I want to drive my body around), an accident breathtaking in its approach, arrives at last to slow me way the fuck down. Ciara's dancing speeds up and slows down the known world in its claim on global time, New York's autumn

splashed against this life
measured out in miles
per hour, to say nothing
of its explication in gallons
of oil. To ride breezily against the backdrop
of huge cost, to endorse its rush as you
fall into it, to drop low like Ciara,
below the adoring skies
of the Hudson Valley
on a Multistrada 1200 the color
of Ludacris's sunglasses in the *Ride* video,
tempering agency via a touchdown
at the 2009 Super Bowl
yet smashed into the wall
of Ciara's poetics of speed
he is hurled toward,
incapable of seeing it
before him. Listening
to Ludacris, I feel flung at her, too,
like we're riding a Ducati into fall,
and, suddenly, we slam
into the season's shifting weather
and are released
into the beige, yellow, and red
of autumn, pastels that sunset over us,

foundering in a haze at the horizon veering from greenish blue to purple like money burning in your hands.

Later, Ciara and I meet in a semidarkened vacant mall and wander through various shops until we find a somewhat new JCPenney, swept up in creamsicle light.

When we enter the department store, it turns out that Ciara and I are together the 10,000th customer and have won a Ducati motorcycle of our choice. It's a spectacular moment, one christened by confetti as Ciara leans over in her fur to accept the hand of the JCPenney employee who congratulates us. Muzak elaborates the celebratory atmosphere of the empty department store, where no one is celebrating, at the moment of our win. I blush as I realize that here I am, with Ciara, pop star unfixed to a music that would determine her, like really it's all pretty plastic in its one-size-fits-all quality, and though she's in love with her beau Future, she's in love with me, too. The JCPenney manager greets us and leads us to the back lot of the department store, into the cool breeze of a late October night, where there are ten bikes lined up, each glinting in the street light. Ciara selects the Multistrada 1200 and says, "This is the one."

"I love it," I tell her. The manager smiles and removes a contract from his suit pocket. He unfolds it and hands it to us. I don't spend any time reviewing the endless pages of terms and conditions and sign immediately. He hands over the keys and the deed to the Multistrada 1200.

Ciara mounts the bike, which, at that moment, doesn't *not* feel like me, and asks me to climb on. Where should we go? she asks. I can hardly speak. This moment becomes a second dream in which I imagine where I might go, out of here, so that even when I do shake myself out of it I can't let go. I remember seeing a Ducati two falls ago on Canal before joining my friends below a moment sparkling in the presence of

the Goldman Sachs employees
who toasted our protest
as the actualized politics
of community eroded
downtown's teary sense
of its ensconced
kingdom, like
we got it, OK,

you don't want this to end,
but we do, even though in a sense
the end brought about a separate
conflict anterior to its original:
how to continue
and still be friends. On Canal,
I spotted a man on a Ducati motorcycle,
perhaps a banker or some other agent
of wealth beyond reproach,
and thought of all gross injustices served
us this, the rich white guy on his bike,
was some reminder of the fault line
that might eventually open up
to swallow him down. If histories
go fast they go faster when compelled
toward an inevitable terminus
made finally realer
in the earnest wish for its sudden
arrival, this delicate
egg of relations I'd like to hurl
at a riot cop's helmet. The Ducati
looped in steel a black, cold ring
I would place on my own finger
but can't because I make
pretty much nothing
and can scarcely afford the rent
of my Crown Heights apartment
let alone a motorcycle

for $15k. Ciara is right: we are each our own Ducati, molded into the steel frame into which we can lean, one night in fall, to ride you, all the bodies upon whom one rides, impaled by such disasters as the sudden recognition that you can't stand to look away, caught in the remaining sunlight, and yet must.

THOMAS SAYERS ELLIS

Conspiracy Simile [A Poet's Guide to the Assassination of JFK and the Assassination of Poetry]

Every poet assassinates poetry.
—Steryl Flexum

Air Force One
American Rifleman
Acoustic Evidence
Agent Provocateurs
Anti Castro Cubans
Arlington National
Cemetery
Assassination Records
Review Board
Autopsy
Autopsy Photos
Autopsy Photos (Altered)
A Mother in History
Babushka Lady
Back Brace
Badge Man
Judyth Vary Baker
Guy Bannister
Barber's *Adagio for Strings*
The Bay of Pigs
Bell & Howell 414PD
Bethesda Naval Hospital
Big Oil
Lem Billings
Lee Bowers

Yaddo
American Poetry Review
Laurie Anderson
Acentos
Cave Canem
AWP

The Paris Review

Diving into the Wreck
Disembodied Poetics
Exquisite Corpse
The World's Wife
Star Black
Back Issues
William Logan
Lee Ann Brown
Ron Silliman
Come on All You Ghosts
Furious Flower
Sad Little Breathing Machine
"After great pain, . . ."
The Nobel Prize
Mistress Bradstreet
Jake Adam York

"brains and eggs"
Madeline Duncan Brown
Mae Brussell
George H. W. Bush
CIA
CIA's National Photographic
Interpretation Center
Earle and Elizabeth Cabell
Cabinet Plane Over the
Pacific
Camelot
  The President
  The First Lady
  Caroline Kennedy
  John F. Kennedy, Jr.
The Carousel Club
Casket, Bronze Ceremonial
Casket, Metal Shipping
Fidel Castro
Rose Cheramie
". . . chickens coming
  home to roost . . ."
Civil Air Patrol
Command Center/
Collins Radio Secret
  Communications
John and Nellie
  Connally
John Connally's Stetson
John Connally's Wounds
Conspiracy Realists
Conspiracy Theorists
Counterfeit Agents
Coup D'etat
The Cover-Up

Contributor's Bio
Madame Deluxe
Grace Cavalieri
The Yale Younger
PSA (Poetry Society of America)
Kinkos

Guns N' Roses
The Cloud Corporation

Faber
Lancer
Lace
Lyric
Lark
Best American Poetry
First Edition
Second Printing
Amiri Baraka
Chelsey Minnis
Frank X Walker

The Necessary Angel
Unterberg Poetry Center/
92nd Street Y

Kingsley and Kate Tufts

Paul Muldoon's *Rackett*
"Four Quartets"
Harriet
Scarriet
Contest Judges
o blek b'ilat
L=A=N=G=U=A=G=E

Crescent City Garage
Walter Cronkite
Cry of Battle (film)
Dallas
Dallas Council on World
  Affairs
Dallas Police
Dallas Police Department
  Basement
Dallas Secret Underground
The Dal-Tex Building
The Dallas Morning News
The Dark Complected Man
George Bannerman Dealey
Dealey Plaza
  31 Motionless People
"The Decision to Go to the
  Moon"
Deep Politics/Deep Throat
Dog Man
"Don't Go to Texas!"
  Reverend Billy Graham
Doorway Man
007 Novels/Ian Fleming
Double Arrest (Oswald)
18 ½ Minute Gap
"The Elderly Negro"
Thomas Eli Davis III
Elm Street "X"
The Epileptic
The Eternal Flame
Amos Lee Euins
Exit Debris Frames
Judith Exner
FBI

GRANTA
Robert Pinsky
louderARTS
The Triggering Town
The William Samuel Livingston Chair

Publishers Weekly
Busboys & Poets

Clebo Rainey & Naomi
Atheneum Books
Words in the Mourning Time (1970)
The Dark Room Collective
George Ames Plimpton
Page
Poetry Reading Audience
Lila Bell Wallace

Best-Selling Jewish Porn Films
Seth Abramson
"Ballistics"
Billy Collins
Dean Young
Movie-Going (1962)
DoubleTake
Untitled
The Book of Negro Folklore
Thomas Sayers Ellis
Scansion
Performance Poet
Robert Frost
Afaa Jess Dawes
Best American Experimental Writing
"Hanky-Panky"
*Inner Voices (1963-2003) /Paper Trail
  (1965-2003)*

Fair Play for Cuba
Committee
Fake Defectors Program
Fake Secret Service Badges
False Leads
David Ferrie
"Fiddle and Faddle"
544 Camp
Forgive My Grief
Free Masons
Jim Garrison
Grassy Knoll
Grassy Knoll Trolls
The Great Society
Agents Greer and Kellerman
Bobby W. Hargis
Van Heflin
The Hertz Clock
Alek James Hiddell
Agent Clint Hill
Jean Hill
James Hood
Hotel Del Charro
Hotel Texas
J. Edgar Hoover
Father Oscar Huber
Sarah T. Hughes
Humes and Boswell
E. Howard Hunt
Illuminati
"I am just a patsy!"
Lyndon Johnson (LBJ)

LBJ's Box 13
LBJ's Psychiatrist

VONA

The Baffler
Bakeless Literary Publication Prizes
Small Press Distribution
David Ferry
Myra Breckinridge
826 Valencia
4 Volumes of Elegies
Free Verse
New Directions
Stage
Wilde Boys
Po Biz
Poets & Writers
Craig M. Teicher
James Franco
Noonday
Persona Poem
"The art of losing isn't hard to master."
Mrs. Giles Whiting
On the Bus with Rosa Parks
The Library Hotel
Tin House
Richard Howard
Padre Spencer Reese
Selected Poems
Orr and Burt
TR Hummer
Lannan
Mexico City Blues
James H. Billington (Librarian
of Congress)
MLA Joblist 2013
Robert N. Casper

Lady Bird Johnson
The Joint Chiefs of Staff
Vivian Malone Jones
JFK's Brain
JFK, Jr.'s Funeral Salute
Jacqueline Kennedy
Joseph P. Kennedy
Rose F. Kennedy

Kennedy Compound
Kennedy Half Dollar
The Kennedy-Johnson
 Ticket
Nikita Khrushchev
Malcolm Kilduff
Dorothy Kilgallen
The Kill Castro Medical
 Team
The Kill Zone
Henry Kissinger

Klein's Sporting Goods
Mary Jo Kopechne
Lamb Chop Puppet
Mark Lane
Life (Magazine)
John Liggett
Evelyn Lincoln
Raymond Loewy
Lone Nut
Lone Nutters
Love Field
Billy Lovelady
"Maggie's Drawers"
The Magic Bullet
Marilyn Mailer

Barbara "MacBird" Garson
FSG
On the Bus with Rosa Parks
Received Forms
Page Number
Cate Marvin
Ulysses
Ariel
The Fine Arts Work Center
The Threepenny Review
The Prolific and the Devourer

Peter Sellers
Harold Augenbraum
Alice Quinn
Callaloo

Index of First Lines
"Huffy Henry hid the day,/
 unappeasable Henry sulked."
Ploughshares
Government Girl
Anaphora
Mark Strand
Ways of Seeing
Thomas Lynch
"Cut the last line"
D.A. Levy
IOWA
The World According to Jorie
The MacDowell Colony
William Corbett
Marjorie Perloff
The Pulitzer Prize
Norman Monroe

William Manchester
James Meredith
Cord Meyer
Mary Pinchot Meyer
Military Industrial
Complex
Eisenhower Warning
Willie Mitchell
Minsk Radio Factory
MKULTRA
The Mob
George de Mohrenschildt
Mary Moorman
Mary Moorman Photo

David Sanchez Morales
Moscow–Washington
Hotline
Motorcade
Motorcade Route
Motorcade Route (Altered)
Bill Moyers
Clint Murchison, Sr.
The Murchison Mansion
"My God, they are going
to kill us all"
The National Archives
Howard Nemerov

The New Frontier
New Orleans, Louisiana
The Newman Family
9/11 Commission Report
1961 Lincoln Continental
4-door Convertible with

William Matthews
On the Bus with Rosa Parks
C.D. Wright
Forrest Gander
BOMB

The Cantos
Mitchell Douglass
text*sound*
CK Williams
Poetry Foundation
Askold Melnyczuk
Rona Jaffe Foundation
Bedtime for Democracy
(The Dead Kennedys)
David Tomas Martinez
KGB Bar

Wave Poetry Bus
"The Road Not Taken"
As the World Turns
The Language of Life: A Festival of Poets
Steven Barclay
All the Vice President's Men
Lit Crit

The Strand Bookstore
Poet Laureate Consultant in Poetry
to the Library of Congress, 1963–64
The Internet
Marfa, Lannan
The New School
Poetry Writing Sample, 571 pages
Ford's (Motor Company) Theater

Jump Seats	
Limousine Bubble Top	Heroic Couplet
Limousine Complete Stop	
Limousine Right Rear Tail Light	*The Autobiography of Red*
Limousine Windshield	Structural Integrity
Richard Nixon	*A Local Storm* (1963)/*Departures* (1973)
Nurse's Classroom	Bluestockings
(at PMH)	
Jackie O	Sharon Olds
Jackie O's Rose	2 oz white rum, ½oz lime juice, 1 dash Cointreau orange liqueur, 1 tsp sugar.
Silvia Odio	Silvana Straw
Oil Depletion Allowance	"Sympathy for the Devil"
"One of your guys did it."	*Meditation In An Emergency*
Aristotle Onassis	*Antaeus*
Orville Nix	Paul Simon
Orville Nix Film	"The Sounds of Silence" (1964)
Orville Nix Film (Altered)	"The Sound of Silence" (1965)
Operation Mongoose	*Brutal Imagination*
Operation 40	*The Great Zoo And Other Poems*
Lee Harvey Oswald	Spoken Word
Harvey	Bob Holman
Lee	Miguel Algarin
(O. H. Lee)	*Libra*
ONI (Office of Naval Intelligence)	AGNI
Marguerite Oswald	Martha Rhodes
Marguerite Oswald	Martha Collins
Marina Oswald	Anne Waldman
Oswald's Bent Firing Pin	&
Oswald's Palm Print	Concrete Poetry

Michael Paine
Ruth Paine
Parkland Memorial Hospital
Parkland Surgeons
The Patsy
The Pedestal

Penn Jones, Jr.
The Pentagon
Pepsi Cola Convention
Jose Perdomo
Permindex
David Atlee Phillips
Photograph of LBJ
Being Sworn In
Photograph of Oswald
Holding Rifle
Photograph of Oswald
Being Shot
Picket Fence
Pink Chanel Suit
Pink Chanel Suit (Blood
Stained)
Pink Pillbox Hat
The Plumbers (1971)
Kenneth Porter (Marina's
Second Husband)
Power Control Group

Freddie Prinze
Profiles in Courage
Project Freedom
The Queen Mary
RFK
The Enemy Within

Kevin Killian
Dodie Bellamy
MFA Program
Graduate Writing Workshop
Howl
Sunday Book Review
(*The New York Times*)
PEN American Center
The Penguin Group
Graywolf Press
Willie Perdomo
Poets House
David Meltzer
In Plato's Cave

Imagism

Unit of Sound/Unit of Meaning

Fence
VIDA
VIDA

Tender Buttons
Foetry
"Land of the Crippled Snake"

The Princeton Encyclopedia of Poetry and Poetics
Miguel Piñero
George
Lighthead Off & Split
Mary Oliver
Nick Flynn
Blind Huber

Dan Rather
The Camera Never Blinked
Real and Retimed Footage
Reily Coffee Company
Red Bird Airport Incident
Rifle(s)
Rifle Report
Rifle Switch
William "Rip" Robertson
Roses, Red (Dallas)
Roses, Yellow (Forth Worth)
Jack Ruby
Jack Ruby's Dog
Charles Senseney
Secret Service
Shadow Government
Clay Shaw
Sirhan Sirhan
Marilyn Sitzman
The Sixth Floor Window
63 Inman Street
Sniper and Spotter
Sniper's Nest
SS 100 X
State Funeral of John F. Kennedy
Steel Strike/Crisis
Stemmons Freeway Sign
Oliver Stone
The Storm Drain
Cecil Stoughton
Sturgis
Frank

Dan Chiasson
The Afterlife of Objects

Leaping Poetry
Coffee House Press
Flying Object
The Lyric "I"/The "I" of the Lyric
Starred Review
Plagiarism
William "Bill" Corbert
Blue Flower Arts
"The Yellow Rose of Texas"

David Lehman
Guest Editor
Cynthia Krupat
National Book Foundation
The Amy Lowell Traveling Scholarship
CAConrad
Shivani Shivani
Tree Swenson
Parnassus
31 Inman Street
Grant Application Deadline
A Public Space
Saratoga Piper PA-32R-301
". . . a formal feeling comes–"

Shut Up Shut Down
The Freedom of Information Act
Brian Turner
Low-Residency
Let Us Now Praise Famous Men
Frank
Sinatra

James Tague

Televised Murder (?) of Oswald
Texas
Democrats of Texas
(DOT)
Texas Regulars
Texas School Book
Depository
Texas Theater
Helen Thomas
Officer J.D. Tippet
Three Assassination
Weekend
Three Spent Cartridges
The Three Tramps
"This t-shirt is unfair"
Clyde Tolson
Top Ten Record Shop
Tina Towner
Tracheotomy
Dr. Janet Travell
Treason Leaflets

Triangulation
Triple Underpass
The Tunnels Under Dallas
Three-Week Cancer
12 noon–1 pm
UFO Files
The Umbrella
Umbrella Man
The Umbrella System

The United States House

". . . is like a villain with a smiling
cheek,"
Who Shot J.R.?/Who J.R. Shot?
Amazon.com
Unsolicited Manuscripts

Simultaneous Submissions
Dodge Poetry Festival

City Lights
Catalog Copy, Print and Electronic
Tony Hoagland
3 Sections

Five Metaphysical Poets
ABC, CBS, NBC
The New Yorker
The Pleasure of the Text
Split This Rock
Tina Brown Celona
Tsvetaeva
Collected Poems
Broadsides/Courtesy of the Center
for Book Arts
The Collected Works of Billy the Kid
Lyrical Ballads
The Tenure Track
Writer's Block
"Skunk Hour"
Slush Pile
Bread Loaf Writer's Conference
Michael Collier
Waiters, Fellows, Scholars,
Faculty & Guests
The Poetry Project at St. Mark's Church

of Representatives	
Select Committee on	
Assassinations (HSCA)	
Jack Valenti	*Protect and Defend (1992)*
Vietnam	Squaw Valley
Wernher von Braun	Franz Wright
Malcolm Wallace's	Found Poetry
Fingerprint	
War is Hell (film)	National Poetry Slam Championship
Warren Commission	Academy of American Poets
Earl Warren	Robert Penn Warren
Richard Russell, Jr	Richard Eberhart
(D-Georgia)	
John Sherman Cooper	Daniel Hoffman
(R-Kentucky)	
Hale Boggs	Reed Whittemore
(D-Louisiana)	
Gerald Ford	William Meredith
(R-Michigan)	
Allen Dulles (former	Allen Tate
Director of the CIA)	
John J. McCoy (former	Robert Fitzgerald
President of the	
World Bank)	
Arlen Specter	Dana Gioia
(Assistant Counsel)	
Warren Commission Report	*Self-Portrait in a Convex Mirror*
Washington	National Endowment for the Arts
Watergate	*The Book of Nightmares* (1973)
White House	Playboy Mansion
The White Oak Cliff(s)	of Dover Beach
White Russian Community	*On Grief and Reason/Dancing in*
	Odessa/Factory of Tears
Witnesses	*The Nation*
Disappearing Witnesses	Out of Print Titles

Witness Testimonies
Abraham Zapruder
The Zapruder Film
The Zapruder Film (Altered)
JFK

Uncorrected Proof
Joseph Campbell
The Hero with a Thousand Faces
The Power of Myth
You Us A

BRYCE EMLEY

The *Panthera tigris*

—from "The Tyger" by William Blake & Merriam-Webster's Online Dictionary

Large Asian carnivorous mammal (*Panthera tigris*) of the cat family having a usually tawny coat transversely striped with black! Large Asian carnivorous mammal (*Panthera tigris*) of the cat family having a usually tawny coat transversely striped with black! giving off light : shining, glowing illustriously, gloriously
In the dense growths of trees and underbrush covering large tracts of the time from dusk to dawn when no sunlight is visible,
What exempt from death terminal part of the vertebrate forelimb when modified (as in humans) as a grasping organ or specialized light-sensitive sensory structure of animals that in nearly all vertebrates, most arthropods, and some mollusks is the image-forming organ of sight
Could shape, construct thy causing or likely to cause fear, fright, or alarm especially because of dangerous quality beauty of form arising from balanced proportions?

In what situated at a greatdistance : far-off oceans or upper atmospheres or expanses of space that constitute apparent great vaults or arches over the earth
Consumed fuel and gave off heat, light, and gases the phenomenon of combustion manifested in light, flame, and heat of thine specialized light-sensitive sensory structures of animals that in nearly all vertebrates, most arthropods, and some mollusks are the image-forming organs of sight?
On what means of flight or rapid progress dare he ascend, soar?
What the terminal part of the vertebrate forelimb when modified (as in humans) as a grasping organ dare take hold of : clutch the phenomenon of combustion manifested in light, flame, and heat?

And what laterally projecting part of the human body formed of the bones and joints with their covering tissue by which the arm is connected with the trunk, and what skill acquired by experience, study, or observation

Could wring or wrench so as to dislocate or distort the tendons of thy hollow muscular organ of vertebrate animals that by its rhythmic contraction acts as a force pump maintaining the circulation of the blood?
And at or during the time that : while thy hollow muscular organ of vertebrate animals that by its rhythmic contraction acts as a force pump maintaining the circulation of the blood set about the activity of : started to pulsate, throb,
What inspiring awe terminal part of the vertebrate forelimb when modified (as in humans) as a grasping organ? and what inspiring awe terminal part of the vertebrate leg upon which an individual stands?

What the hand tool consisting of a solid head set crosswise on a handle and used for pounding? what the series of usually metal links or rings connected to or fitted into one another and used for various purposes (as support, restraint, transmission of mechanical power, or measurement)?
In what enclosed structure in which heat is produced (as for heating a house or for reducing ore) had, maintained, or occupied a place, situation, or position thy portion of the vertebrate central nervous system enclosed in the skull and continuous with the spinal cord through the foramen magnum that is composed of neurons and supporting and nutritive structures (as glia) and that integrates sensory information from inside and outside the body in controlling autonomic function (as heartbeat and respiration), in coordinating and directing correlated motor responses, and in the process of learning?
What the heavy usually steel-faced iron block on which metal is shaped (as by hand hammering)? what inspiring awe handle
Dare its likely to cause or capable of producing death frightening aspects seize with or as if with the hand : grasp?

At or during the time that : while the natural luminous bodies visible in the sky especially at night propelledthroughthe air by a forward motion of the hand and arm toward or in a lower physical position their thrusting or throwing weapons with long shafts and sharp heads or blades,
And moistened, sprinkled, or soaked with water the expanse of space that seems to be over the earth like a dome : firmament with their drops of clearsalinefluid secreted by the lacrimal gland anddiffusedbetween the eye

and eyelids to moisten the parts and facilitate their motion,
Did he have, produce, or exhibit a smile his something produced or accomplished by effort, exertion, or exercise of skill to perceive by the eye?
Did he who brought into being by forming, shaping, or altering material : fashioned the Young Sheep bring into being by forming, shaping, or altering material : fashion thee?

Large Asian carnivorous mammal (*Panthera tigris*) of the cat family having a usually tawny coat transversely striped with black! Large Asian carnivorous mammal (*Panthera tigris*) of the cat family having a usually tawny coat transversely striped with black! giving off light : shining, glowing illustriously, gloriously
In the dense growths of trees and underbrush covering large tracts of the time from dusk to dawn when no sunlight is visible,
What exempt from death terminal part of the vertebrate forelimb when modified (as in humans) as a grasping organ or specialized light-sensitive sensory structure of animals that in nearly all vertebrates, most arthropods, and some mollusks is the image-forming organ of sight
Could shape, construct thy causing or likely to cause fear, fright, or alarm especially because of dangerous quality beauty of form arising from balanced proportions?

ADAM FITZGERALD

"Time After Time"

I'm in the barricade hearing the clock thickening you.
   Autumn encircles a confusion that's nothing new.
Flashback to warring eyes almost letting me drown.

Out of which, a picture of me walking in a foreign head.
   I can't hear what you said. Then you say: Cold room
(the second that life unwinds). A tinctured vase returns

to grass. Secrets doled out deep inside a drumbeat out
   of tune. Whatever you said was ghostly slow like
a second hand unwinding by match-light. Lying back

to the wheel, I shirked confusion. You already knew.
   Suitcases surround me. You picture me far ahead.
Yet I can't hear what you've said. You say: Doldrums,

have some secondhand wine. Love knew my precincts.
   The stone house turned black and the scenic tunics
were deep inside. Who said home? Oh, I fall behind.

That very secret height blinds. Lying like a diamond,
   the cock-thickening of you: hunchbacked arms, eyes
left behind. You'll picture me walking far, far ahead.

I hear what you've done. You said: Go slow. I feebly
   bleed out. Matthew's sermon turned out to be glass.
I wander in windows soft as Sour Patch. No rewind.

But something is out of touch and you're Sinbad.
   The second date was mine. In a private vacuum,
the thickening plot thinks of you. The future knew.

TOUCHDOWN. Lights. All those celebrity behinds.
   Suitcase full of weeds. You picture me coming to.
You: too close to me to hear what you've already said.

Then you say: The second wind unwinds. Doves whistle,
   halving their dovely backs, watching windows to see
if I'm okay. See it, the dulcet moment? I'm like thicket

tinkering for you. Fusion nothing new. Flashback to
   seagull-beguiled eyes. Sometimes talking to a barren
lad. Such music so unbearably droll. The hand is mine.

Random picture-frames off the darkness. A Turing machine?
   Scotch-Taping through windows, stolen from deep inside
rum-beaded thyme. You say also: Behind sequins & hinds . . .

And I'm in the barricade hearing the clock thickening you.
   Clematis enclosures, walking with news, pollinated by
a secondary grief while something reminds you of our love.

SESSHU FOSTER

Movie Version: "Hell to Eternity"

Guy Gabaldon, born in 1926 and raised in East L.A., shined shoes on skid row from the age of ten. At twelve, he moved in with the Nakano family of Boyle Heights, where he learned Japanese. When the Nakanos were sent to camps in Arizona, 17 year old Gabaldon joined the marines and used "backstreet Japanese" to capture 1,500 Japanese troops on Saipan. In the movie version, he was played by a white actor named Jeffrey Hunter, who suffered a stroke at age 42 in 1969 and died falling down the stairs.

In the movie version, skid row was played by 1960s Bunker Hill and age 12 was played by a grasshopper flying in a summer field. Sweetness careened down the streets in buses and trolleys.

In the movie version, a ten year old boy shining shoes was played by Route 66 and the relocation camps were played by cars going by. Packards were played by Dodges.

In the movie version, the cold beer is played by country music nasal twang, and Jeffrey Hunter was played by slight nausea and nostril flare. His headache was played by the 20th century.

In the movie version, the actual colors of the rushing ocean were played by a whirr of a strip through the machine and the sizzling palm leaves were played by folded taco smell. Somebody was played by nobody.

In the movie version, the present is played by an off-camera past with seagulls added or removed and palm trees painted on a canvas backdrop of night. Popcorn smell was played by cotton candy.

In the movie version, wishes were played by a voice over of broken dishes and bouts of influenza were played by old magazines in the back. Smoke in a funnel over the hills was played by extras dressed like citizens.

In the movie version, East L.A. was played by the blood bursting an artery and dust specks thrown into a ray on the stairs. The golden moment balking.

C. S. GISCOMBE

4 and 5 from "Early Evening"

4.

Went downtown to see

the new King Kong. Lost track of time but I kept walking—

landmarks fell into order and I held my pace among them. Where do

you go to think about anything? Early show, just another

ten or fifteen minutes.

What was the Commonwealth to me?

(Twenty-five townships to Centre County—the lines

follow the contour of ridges and valleys—and therein the creeks are runs; or

colored Bellefonte, above Spring Creek which, in the borough, forms the
boundary

—colored Bellefonte on its hill facing Catholic

Bellefonte, across Spring Creek.) Coffee-town is burning down! Where

you been, Charlie Brown?

Skull Island.

Knock, knock!

Four is a door, some

sour pranks over and over again.

I'll go on ahead, I thought, after all I'm Mister Schism. Four's

the answer and the exit too.

5.

Or hell's in this one particular part of heaven, once you know

that you are, as it were, "in the car." A main street branches, typically,

in some towns, like a hand. Something I did, something

I can do. But five is a hive, baby—a-buzz, bee-loud,

tingling with consequence, anything

you want. Where was I? Downtown. (Now you see it and then you're

there.) In spades, a measure parallel to everything—as though

there were a fête going on and we'd left the car

to flirt with the organizers. Where was I, Charlie Brown?

I've met the Catholics too and I've been to the rural campuses

of Penn State, small-town schools for the greatest part

devoid of black students. The main campus at University Park was
beautiful with

its walks shaded by the elm trees, the tops of which are lit and merge,
    in early evening,

with roofs of the old stone buildings to make a single sky-line. Where

had I been going? To a séance, apparently. It was dusk

when we set out.

RENEE GLADMAN

Number Two of the Eleven Calamities

I made a shape by placing a figure inside a word and pushing the word off the page, so that in my mind and in the mind of anyone reading that page, anyone who knew the language in which I was writing, which at that time was English, would be able to change that plane of language into some picture of living that had a time and a place and objects different from the picture that was the world of the body writing but resembling it, too, and this picture, which was hard to share with other people, who were not also reading or writing that page in which words were being pushed into being—this picture could play and pause at will. It could not play or pause separate from the mind of the body that was typing in that familiar world, where a cup of tea was growing cold, but it could play and pause in the way that the world bearing the cup could not. I sat down with the objective of pushing words off the page and bringing a picture into being and doing this for a number of hours in a row, for a number of days, all accumulating into a number of months, perhaps amounting to years, such that this became a picture in which was embedded many other pictures and that gave off a dimensional feeling, even though these pictures belonged to my thinking and were nestled in my mind, which like everything else in thought was not like a pot you could pick up and pour water in and warm up but rather was like seeing a pot and imagining all the actions therein. You made a space that gathered all the possible pictures that could be accreted through all of the pushing of words off the page into a void space, quickly being filled with pictures. I sat the cup down. I pushed the words "I sat the cup down" off the page, then picked up the cup and sat it down. I drank from the cup, though I didn't remember that act for days. I only remembered that I drank when I read the words on a page before the page became a picture with a body standing at a window above cars parking below. But, I couldn't long think about what I could take into my mouth at that time of day and what my body needed before I was understanding that all the cars were parking at the same time, and this was strange. It never happened this way. You never had a moment where every car on one street was parking at once; you never had a street where all the cars had been gone then returned all at once, all wanting to park and all finding a space to park and to park at the same time as all the others. Wherever it was that I was standing provided me a vantage point in which the information that I gathered was becoming a problem for the picture that held me. I had to grab another picture and append it to this one, so that I didn't get stuck, perpetually sipping from that cup and looking over cars behaving bizarrely. But, how could I find my way out of this picture without returning to that page and a new line of words to push into another space to bring me, not here—no longer to this space—but to the next space that answered the problem of the time of day where whole neighborhoods return at once and park their cars then all go into the same house.

MAGGIE GLOVER AND ISAAC PRESSNELL

Email Exchange

Hey there! Okay, how about this:

1. We each send each other a poem that we wrote during our first year of grad school.

2. Once we receive the poem, we choose ambient language from some music or a show or movie or book or article. We copy down snippets of that language to later combine with the poem.

3. We take each other's poem, cut it up into phrases that we feel have their own "weight" that we find interesting (obviously subjective, but I think that's okay).

4. We reassemble the phrases randomly, accompanied by phrases from the secondary source (intentionally or unintentionally . . . we might have to just wait and see what happens.)

6. We send each other the "finished" poem.

What do you think? I know that this might be more controlled than a true chance operation (I think my preference to be in charge is showing through here . . .)

Hey!

I think that's perfect. Part of me thinks it might be interesting to go a little deeper, although I hesitate to suggest this. What if we broadened the scope and worked with poems we wrote during the whole trajectory of our romantic relationship. I know it might seem like a cruel project, but it could also be really interesting/ fruitful. What do you think?

Hi,

So, by "the whole trajectory of our romantic relationship," do you mean from the time we met our first year of grad school, through the infidelity and breakup, through the aftermath and the ways we continued to hurt each other, ending with graduation when we went our separate ways and didn't speak again for some years? ;)

Haha, yup. That's what I mean.

Like a Flock of Tiny Birds

I.

Three thousand miles away, oh sweetie,
paint each other's faces, reminiscences.
Fuck this and conceal two clowns
in my brain, our families again between realism
and romanticism, convenient theories.
That heartless art, I like to say.
You're a good person
loose inside me, the knoll
to explain touch again because I can't.
Dad, you've begun calling him names.
I bring non-threatening boy on a blanket
if I could, some kind of scrim.
Our fathers don't touch me.
We're talking about no wonder, kicking
obligatory facts where I sit, city of San Francisco.
He never got married. From the dark,
things as they really were went red.
Our lives had a retired circus, his damp
hands to separate around the eyes,
back and forth about our friendship,
to us, recently, bright colors, features
of my mother. We each want an old friend.
I'm here, the whole god like a hacky sack
to remember the other, reliving when I grew
to see city. I'd forgotten the dark. I would
show him to the park in bold. How I, did I
let so easily. Technically, I didn't.

II.

Besides the smoke of affection scattered around us,
can't you see I'm of the fireplace? I had your skin.
In their kitchen, something had changed
on the checkered tile. Words start to hurt in a big house.
I dream *Love you, cunt* with cathedral ceilings.
I drank too much. Magnavox in the basement,
radioactive isotopes, stained glass windows,
his own life going for an ice pick, for any
tenderness, a backyard pond. Lucky, aren't we?
The splintered patio pressed against the wrought iron.
Dad's cigars, the clothes he tells I am. And thus
I can describe jumbled up, smell like the patio.
Thus he is asking to make him hate from this coast
like puppets hung, tiny dead turtles, some sign
of Mom's candles, of the old stupid pattern.
What if I grew up thinking about his drink?
And so the hum, turn-key to stir what does.

III.

Slices of brain refused to touch and deflate.
Unevenly, briefly, our knees touched,
and forgotten sucks in the sun's reflection.
The last picture of us, so I sink in. I was being
swallowed, accidentally stored. I'd pretend
at the beach all these years: leftover lasagna,
Papa's bloodied napkins, a breaking wave,
in with mine, in the crisper, scissors and a steady
hand from here to there, beneath plastic wrap
because they were mine. The heat of another
holds my feet captive. Debts and men to be sent.
Ice blue eyes like oil trapped, ashamed of the sand,

the needs placed over Father's death, mucousy
woodiness, a cooler further. Jellyfish dry.
Longing for what happened, pink from the sun.

IV.

Below the heart, children crave routine.

When the first boy showed disconnect,
I slammed my fist. There was a blackout
with a pocket knife in a file marked "business."
Like a maranka gourd, the musty loneliness
and a wad of gum. My thoughts in order
of appearance. Against his ear, I had
composed an answer, stuck on my locker
paintings about sexism. The school nurse called,
echoing through, confused. MG carved repetition
of the breastbone. *You're a big girl.*
I was thirteen, perennial memory, which bloated,
but I relish that he cared. The doctor says
how to aim *I'm sorry*. Dad had an affair
or a junkie child molester who showed me
into his arm. Refracted through this, my father
for the middle, if he knew his own child.

V.

Along with their hosts, world of the unwell,
malignants cut out and other so-called "invasives,"
the pancreatitis with the only thing, a teetotaler's
warning. *He loved you so much* treated with pills,
the wake of his seeming removed from the spine.
I still remember the bleeding. Ulcers are shrunken
and primordial. The clogged ones don't cry,

grafted into *yes, godammit*, benign tumors.
Of childhood friendship, we are talking
with wide, black eyes again and again.
On the last night when we talk, he asked for
recycled arteries. When I was a little girl, they cut
open about money. My father of birthmarks
nestled back inside, poor Mom about him.

VI.

I could hear them inside, sponging up
loaded suitcases, talking about mortgage rates
while snow began—high noon of our story.
Cooked in the kitchen, my boyfriend picked me
without kissing me up in the morning, blameless
as a blade. When I left college—the smell
of thawing peat to break your heart.
Lives turn out: Jeff Tweedy on the radio
between remembering and forgetting,
watching TV, rain on the roof, my father
a kind of pinkish blush. Mother stole
a cigarette. I am trying to cut off her fingers.
I left their home since I'd actually kissed
in the basement for good, sex dream
on the patio while my mother, her child-
bearing hips from my father's pack.
Note to future self: my body disgusts you.
To fall singing into the trunk, any crumb
of pretense smoked it. I've seen it happen.

VII.

Different from regret, at first, to help me
remember my actual thoughts, those big ones,
like an incantation. I can't quite recall
when they found her, being straight
from high school. I've lived within my husband
to the first hurts. I've tried to be good,

its blanket fort, mothers with strollers,
while we try *just be happy*, my glittered shoes
like a guest. Guilt is a state she'd never had
before we talk, Frank Lloyd Wright screwing
the wives, each rejection just the size,
vibrating stones, and then I catastrophize
with the toilet paper. In how long, how it leads
back to dad, to my appointment. I wear
I'm not good. I remember in my hands.
My therapist calls me. Just an operation
about how we'd looked. A pixie,
as it turned. I hold. I'm not going.

VIII.

With corn-colored hair, the girl and her dying cat
frosting as I walk. I have something to tell you
of leather, post-coital brunches, a sense of fumbling
in a hailstorm. I hated in a man & wholesome
cardigans, my mother's breathing about what
my hands could do, about her naïve misery.
Pass out doughnuts. My life could go for a
sparkle fix, dusty abstract paintings, fuck me harder.
I tap my laptop, fingers idly wandering down
to the root. I liked your story with rhinestone eyes
cut in the paper. My father calls like a fist

of shame and guilt, the blood-red stain. I've had
ten legs without rhythm. Some were scrawls.
I wear my teenage legs in the bathroom
to be like this. I wear their words, a gentle
sound she's loved. I tear open my own body.
I tell him the prosthesis has to change,
work my hands, any intention of coming back
from the cabinet. At work, Christmas came and went.
Of each strand, my mind swam into the private lives.
Nice ladies wait for my heart to remind me I cried
until the vacuum finally stopped, taking hold somehow
like Tarkovsky, all the way sorry for him.
I lose myself, hitting the window. My college legs,
smells of cheap disinfectant sweet as buttercream.
Someone to play to where I am. To sleep like
a little girl, a cotton scarf. I know I'm stitched forever
and hang up by six. I lather so little into my palms.
How many showers to go alone? It smells as the cream
on my wrist, of hair dye, of orgasms myself. I'm trying
the hail into my hair in meetings, in some home.
I just want original use, a box, a loop of me.
A turtle ring helps me keep the most me.
I hugged him. This morning jostled awake.

ALEXIS PAULINE GUMBS

"Black Studies" and all its children[1]

Picture the house. The house is spilling. There are hands out the window but the doors have barricades. Picture the hands. The hands are crucial. The hands are eloquent they are spelling back their hair. Picture the hair. The hair is heaping. The hair is helping. The hair will overtake. Picture the help. The help are horrified. Their children are learning to dismantle the state.

---

[1] Hortense Spillers, *Black, White and in Color*, Introduction, 39.

ELIZABETH HALL

from "I Have Devoted My Life to the Clitoris: A History of Small Things"

Female Ejaculation?

- Before the explosion of internet porn, The British Board of Film Classification (BBFC) was responsible for regulating films seeking classification as R18, which meant they could be sold to licensed sex shops. On May 2001, the BBFC passed *Squirt Queens* (retitled *British Cum Queens*) only after excising six minutes and twelve seconds of an actress ejaculating during orgasm. According to the committee, the scene constituted urolagnia, banned since 1959 by the Obscene Publications Act. The BBFC board stated, ". . . expert medical advice informed us that there is no such thing as 'female ejaculation' and that the fluid present in *Squirt Queens* was in fact urine." They did not believe that the film showed female ejaculation because, to them, the very act itself was impossible. Their loss.

- The first pussy I saw up close belonged to an aging barfly named Alana, and it looked nothing like my own. While my cunt was the definition of a slit—long slim lips shoring up a compact clit, puritan in its lack of ornamentation—Alana's pussy was a florid, almost hairless, forest of folds. I wasn't sure what to do when I pushed her panties to the side, how long to continue. I simply licked each fold till they began to wriggle, fan out, then circled back to her clit. She tilted her head, "Ah." And just like that—a clear, briny dew filled my mouth. It was not, as some say, the nectar of gods; more, the gleam at the end of the forest.

- Although I had spent the first twenty or so years of my life unaware that women could ejaculate—or, at least, produce the strong, visible streams so associated with male orgasm—I did not need anyone to explain what had happened with Alana. I did not need to read a book: I was there.

- One of the first thorough studies on the female prostate was published in 1948 by gynecologist John W. Huffman who discovered that the tissue surrounding the urethra contained prostatic-like glands (found in male uretha) near the urethral opening; one model had up to thirty-one glands.

- Named after Dr. Ernst Grafenberg, a German gynecologist, the G-spot was originally thought to be solely responsible for female ejaculation. This view was advanced in the 1982 book *The G-Spot*, which introduced the highly sensitive area to the mainstream; however, as later discovered, ejaculation can accompany any kind of orgasm. Grafenberge wrote, ". . . large quantities of a clear, transparent fluid are expelled not from the vulva, but out of the urethra in gushes."

- In her book *Eve's Secrets: A New Theory of Female Sexuality* (1987), Josephine Sevely documented the extensive history of female ejaculation, arguing that the phenomenon was well-known to societies across the world from antiquity to the 19th century.

- Vladimir Nabokov knew: in his novel *Ada or Ardor*, set in the late 19th century, two teen girls (also sisters) play a game called "pressing the spring" by "interweaving like serpents" and "kissing her *krestik*."

- The *corpus spongiosum*, G-spot, and urethral sponge all refer to the same swath of tissue, which are included in the Federation of Feminist Women's Health Clinic's definition of the "complete clitoris."

- Beverly Whipple and John Perry (1980's) found that many women produce a clear, alkaline fluid that is not urine which may vary in amount from a few drops to about a quarter cup (roughly two ounces), sometimes up to eight ounces. They also found that prostatic acid phosphatase (PAP), an enzyme that is present in male prostatic secretions, and glucose were "substantially higher in the ejaculatory fluid [of women] than in urine samples."

- In 1997 Spanish researchers Francisco Cabello Santamaria and Rico Nesters analyzed the urine of twenty-four women before and after orgasm for the presence of prostate-specific antigen (PSA). Unlike the preograsmic urine samples, seventy-five percent of the postograsmic samples showed a concentration of PSA. In the fluid emitted at the height of orgasm, one hundred percent of the samples contained PSA. All women are capable of ejaculation, but the amount may be too little to notice. Even if they look very close.

- Performer Carol Queen wrote in *Exhibitionism for the Shy* that her ejaculate tasted like buttered popcorn, sometimes the forest floor, while Fanny Fatale reported that hers had no smell.

- A lover once wrote in a poem that I tasted like scorched marmalade, but he was a romantic.

BRECKEN HANCOCK

The Art of Plumbing

3300 BCE: Copper pipes snake beneath an Indus palace. Sewage systems and democratic access to public wells ensure two millennia of peace.

2500 BCE: Nascent plumbers in Mesopotamia experiment with clay mixed into shredded straw. Bitumen tars conduits and stopgap plugs. After finding his brindled whippet drowned in a tub of crude oil, King Gilgamesh orders the first public execution by tar and feather.

2475 BCE: Egyptians install bathing chambers and lavatories in the Abusir tombs. Pharaoh Sahure employs mummified falcons, ibises and cats as water-bearers in the afterlife. The naked mole rat goes blind living exclusively underground.

1795 BCE: To seduce his wife and celebrate their first wedding anniversary, Hephaestus designs a cast-iron talonfoot. Custodian of *techne*, Hephaestus forwards both technique and technology. He is admired as an artist and wright but reviled as a labourer and a cripple. Weeks later, catching Ares at her taps, Hephaestus ensnares the adulterers in the tub's sister invention: an unbreakable chain-link shower curtain, so fine it's invisible.

1200 BCE: The wet dream of immortality. Thetis dips Achilles in the Styx.

1195 BCE: Linear B records an ancient name for the personal bathtub: *re-wo-te-re-jo*. After serving as a ritual fixture, the Larnax tub bears a corpse across the sea to the afterlife. Minoans boast elaborate aqueducts, hot and cold running taps, and sewage systems that accommodate a prototypical flush toilet. They bathe and bury in the same vessel.

1183 BCE: Clytemnestra guts Agamemnon in the bath. His final berth is a skiff fashioned of fingernails pitched down a river of urine. Sky whips him like Clytemnestra's crop of black hair. Albino giants on grave mounds guard the east bank, awaiting redress for the sacrifice of his daughter.

1046 BCE: Warriors of the Zhou Dynasty observe rituals of hair washing to preserve honour in battle. In one famous tale, Confucius visits Lao-tzu while the latter curtains his hair over a scabbard to dry.

603 BCE: King Nebuchadnezzar of Babylon crawls like a vole through the dust. For seven years he lives with beasts, tearing and eating his own skin. God tortures him with dementia, body lice, swampy testicles and incontinence. In every bracken bush he sees a nightjar, the psychopomp's familiar, come to chirr him down to the Great Below. Finally pardoned for his sin of arrogance and allowed to live, he returns to the Hanging Gardens where slaves sluice the filth from his body, scrubbing him with soap congealed from goat blubber and cremation ash.

500 BCE: Ornate baths rise as key fixtures of Roman architecture. Urban citizens daily visit any one of many public thermæ; private balnea in wealthy homes resemble shallow swimming pools and encompass entire rooms. Romans effectively avoid plague by creating a complex sanitation system that hurries sewage from the city in bronze pipes.

350 BCE: The Hohokam, in what is now Arizona, dig trenches and build pipelines using bored-out logs that shuttle irrigation over two hundred miles. Leaks quench slugs, bulbs, berries and weedy fronds. Spotted across the Sonaran Desert, a blotch of javelina cabbage burgeons at every chink.

343 BCE: Nectanebo II, last native ruler of Egypt, flees to Nubia following the Persian invasion, leaving behind what would have been his sarcophagus. Later installed as a ritual bath in a mosque, the green breccia box is inscribed with extracts from the book of Imi-duat, a historical record of kings and priests, not to be confused with the book of Amduat (*That Which Is in the Afterworld*).

232 BCE: Mathematician, astronomer and inventor Archimedes stumbles onto a method for gauging the volume of irregular objects. Stepping into the bath, he spots water rise counter to the submersion of his body. According to rumour, he sprints naked through the streets of Syracuse, proclaiming either 'God has given me the answer!' or '*I* have found it!'

63 BCE: Augustus Caesar commissions an artificial lake, eighteen hundred feet by twelve hundred feet, where criminals and slaves stage *navalia proelia*, simulated sea battles. By Nero's time, theatrical water wars utilize up to nineteen thousand men and over a hundred ships. Drowning bulls dog-paddle through bile-blooming blue, the floating button mushrooms of men's overbrimmed fat, and the chum of their own blood.

28 CE: John the Baptist dips Jesus in the Jordan. From shore, Joseph replays his recurring wet nightmare: Mary becomes pregnant from sperm in the caldarium.

300 CE: Farmers between Ilminster and Bath maintain a sarcophagus as a horse trough. Resting in a backyard garden, the marble fixture depicts the life of Jonah, said to be reborn from the belly of a monster. The front offers three time-lapse engravings: first, Jonah's boat, tossed at sea, awaits the tentacled embrace of Ketos; second, Ketos vomits Jonah onto an island; and finally, the hero reclines safely against a tree hoisting a gourd of mead, his arm around a peacock.

415 CE: Anxious that nudity nurtures licentiousness, early Christian fathers preach against public bathing. Washing is condoned for cleanliness, but not recreation. Extensive renovations convert a Roman bathhouse into the Basilica of Santa Pudenziana—pools become baptismal fonts, lounging benches, pews. The Latin *creatio*, 'creation from nothing,' applies specifically to the potency of God. Architects and other artists are mere imitators or converters, never inventors. Cassiodorus writes, 'Things made and created differ, for we can make who cannot create.'

625 CE: Gaozu, inaugural emperor of the Tang Dynasty, bequeaths his bathing tub as a palace legacy. The tub's engraved aphorism buoys the twenty-two emperors to come with a lesson of change and renovation: 'Every day, make thyself new. Day by day, make thyself new, and new again, and new again, and forever new.'

900 CE: Mayans plumb the first pressurized water feature in the new world and inscribe tubs with an astrological cartography, atlas to the waterways of beyond.

1348 CE: Forty-five percent of Europe's population succumbs to the Black Death. Bathing, thought to transmit disease through the pores of the body, begins to decline as common practice. One hundred and fifty years later, Queen Isabella of Castile boasts at having bathed only twice in her lifetime: once at birth and once on her wedding day.

1611 CE: Hungarian countess Erzsébet Báthory perfects the iron maiden. Over six hundred teenaged virgins wilt in the metal coffin, organs bored, blood spilling out a grate in the bottom. Báthory bathes in their juices to preserve her youth. In one famous story, she consults with King Matthias while fanning her honour over the pillow to dry.

1627 CE: The Witch Trials in Bamberg, Germany, are the most extensive in Europe. Prince-Bishop Gottfried Johann Georg Fuchs von Dornheim establishes a firm of full-time torturers and builds Drudenhaus, a dedicated witch prison to house the special appliances that deal with the damned. Children as young as six months are ritually dunked in ice-cold baths and scorched in tubs of lime. The wealthiest citizens fall victim to the hunt, their assets and property confiscated as Dornheim and his officers grow wealthy and porcine. Although the accused never escape eventual burning at the stake, Dornheim popularizes a pithy slogan by which he justifies the intermediate torture: 'we drown the witch within to let the Christian live.'

1793 CE: With quill and paper in hand, Jean-Paul Marat soaks in a cold tub to soothe the itchy explosions that crater his skin. Charlotte Corday stabs him there, leaving the knife's mast to hoist the red flag of his chest. Marat's vessel, a ship of French Revolutionaries' fingernails, ferries him through the sewers of Paris. Rats with facial tumours sentinel the west bank. Living exclusively underground, they've gone blind.

1843 CE: *Rub-a-tug-tug. Three hung men in a tub.*

1846 CE: Cholera epidemics and the germ theory of contagion lead to the Public Baths and Wash Houses Act in England. Governments provide the working class facilities to keep clothes and bodies clean.

1847 CE: The royal bathing machine, a green weatherboard carriage on large black wheels, is built at Osborne House on the Isle of Wight. Most contraptions of the time are horse-drawn: chestnut-deep in the surf, Clydesdales are brought around to face the shore. Inside the cabana even the most refined female can change into a bathing costume and then descend by a few steps out the back—the machine completely blocking any public view. Queen Victoria's modern ramp-and-winch system, powered by steam engine (and complete with plumbed toilet), allows her to trundle into the shallows and dip while maintaining her modesty. After her first excursion, she confides to her journal: 'Drove to the beach with my maids in the machine. I undressed and bathed in the sea (for the first time in my life!). I thought it delightful till I put my head under water—and thought I would be stifled by all the black water of England.'

1872 CE: The Ku Klux war in North Carolina shuts down the Mars Hill College campus. One KKK ballad, later found hand-scrawled in the college's archives, sneers at Reuben Manning Deaver who reportedly hid in his bathtub to avoid a rub-a-scrub-scrub at the hands of the Klan.

1890 CE: According to an ancient Russian proverb, a woman in a tub is a room within a room. Sponging his wife's pregnant belly, Sergey Malyutin conceives the first matryoshka doll.

1891 CE: No sooner has the bathtub become a fixture in the working-class home than it offers a common altar for suicide. In Halifax, seventeen-year-old Thomas Drake breaks into his neighbours' house to slit his wrists. The Smiths find him alive, reclining in a tub infused with blood, petting their cat Teddy perched on the edge.

1909 CE: Three-hundred-and-forty-pound William Howard Taft becomes lodged in the White House bathtub, nearly missing his inauguration. When the story surfaces in the media years later, Taft's supporters attempt to discredit the rumours by pointing to a revealing symmetry: the President and his Justice Department had dissolved the Bathtub Trust, a cartel of porcelain makers bent on creating a pricefixing monopoly to control the sale of bathtubs and toilets.

1917 CE: Controversy rocks the bathing world when H. L. Mencken publishes a completely inaccurate account of bathing and bathtub history.

1920 CE: Bathtub gin, a vile bootleg solution to prohibition, explodes onto the U.S. market. Homicide rises by 12.7%; battery by 13.2%. John Dillinger bathes in banknotes both before and after bottles of whiskey.

1925 CE: From the froth of her tub, gin in hand, Zelda Fitzgerald hosts the most renowned Hollywood parties. The same year, discovering F. Scott's affair with the silent film actress Lois Moran, Zelda stuffs all her own clothes into the bathtub and sets them afire.

1933 CE: For Pablo Picasso, art augments nature and the artist is a second creator, one unbounded by any law. His paintings are his legacy, his progeny, his immortality. God, he says, is just another artist. And also, 'Everything is a miracle. It's a miracle we don't melt in the bath.'

1984 CE: When his fishing trawler sinks, Guðlaugur Friðþórsson swims six hours in the North Atlantic off the coast of the Westman Islands. Two fellow fishermen die of hypothermia, but 'the miracle man' somehow survives the cold and the Kraken by talking to múkki, seabirds, and unknowingly relying on his seal-like fat, found later to be three times thicker than usual for humans. Finally navigating the cliffs and crawling up onto an ancient lava field, Friðþórsson walks barefoot over two kilometres of terrain. His soles turn to ribbons that unravel across pumice humps of molten rock. He finds a bathtub meant to trough sheep and punches a hole through its ice, finally plunging his face in the fresh water to drink.

1999 CE: In a British Columbia time-share, Diana Yano drowns her five-year-old daughter and her three-year-old son to heaven.

2000 CE: *Pity the bathtub its forced embrace of the human form.*

2002 CE: An eccentric en route to his own wedding travels over one thousand kilometres from Odessa to Kyiv in a motorized bathtub. In the vicinity of Uman, he is trapped for two hours on the roadside, swarmed by a storm of stag beetles.

2003 CE: In his documentary *My Architect*, Nathaniel Kahn explores the secret life of his father, world-renowned architect Louis Kahn, who maintained three different families with three different women. Nath, revealing the truth of his paternity for the first time, lays bare his father's social delinquency, but also honours the artist and visionary. In one section, viewers navigate footage of the Trenton Bath House in New Jersey, a pivotal design Kahn credits as a turning point in his career—'from this came a generative force which is recognizable in every building I've designed since.' Nath pairs the Bath House with an archival audio track of his father:

A work of art is not a living thing that walks or runs, but the making of a life. That which gives you a reaction. To some it is the wonder of man's fingers. To some it is the wonder of the mind. To some it is the wonder of technique. And to some, how real it is. To some, how transcendent it is. Like the Fifth Symphony, it presents itself with a feeling —that you know it, if you've heard it once. And you look for it. Though you know it, you must hear it again.

Though you know it, you must see it again. Truly a work of art is one that tells us Nature cannot make what Man can make.

2007 CE: Tatsuya Ichihashi rips out the bathroom fixtures in his Tokyo sky-rise flat. After beating Lindsay Ann Hawker to death with an amputated faucet, he buries her in a bathtub of sand on his balcony. Weeks later police find her, right fingertips exposed, pinned by weather to the rim.

2011 CE: Two road workers recline in a makeshift hot tub atop a fire fuelled with ruins from the drowned city of Fukushima.

2014 CE: I need to soak. Gathering my spilt hair from the pillow, I rise from the television news, from the *navalia proelia* on our sheets. Grief isn't an epoch; it's a milieu. In the tub, Mom's waiting, water slipping through the noose at its bottom. Tuberous teats in the faucet's bulb. One damp hand fixed to the hot faucet; fingernails chewn, skin leavened at the quick. It's not quick; the earth turns round on its spit.

3300 CE: The untethered husks of our bathyspheres tub to shore and spa like meteors on a lush rub of beach. Fomenting sleep escapes from the slack jaws of their hatches ajar.
No one to breathe; no one to breathe against. My nude feet match the pitching heave of sand, pass the batches of dismembered claws piled like garbage. I only meant to shush you for a node, a nodule in time. Our water births and our burials at sea come to this. *Take my mother, throw her in the ocean. Who should love me, O, like the ocean?* I douche in tsunami; I'm radiant. It's the end of man and I can do whatever I want.

2

TEN LITTLE NIGGA (K)NOTS
AND THEN THERE WERE NONE

3

ANIMATO.
angels
Five little ~~nigga (k)nots~~ leanin' on the subway doors, One tumbled to the tracks then there were four.
pdl.
angels
Four little ~~nigga (k)nots~~ on a snatch-&-grab-knockout spree, One got hit by a hollow point then there were three;
pdl.
angels
Three little ~~nigga (k)nots~~ playin' pick up ball at noon, One tased and cuffed himself then there were two.
pdl.
angels
Two little ~~nigga (k)nots~~ shooting three dice in the sun, One frizzled into a fist then there was one;
pdl.
angels
One little ~~nigga (k)not~~ left all alone, He drove to a clearing and hung him - self then there were none.
pdl.
Then there were none and then there were none; God Bless America then there were none.
pdl.

4

TEN LITTLE ANGELS
LET'S COUNT THEM ALL AGAIN!

5

ANIMATO.
afro puffs
Six little ~~angels~~ buying snacks at 7-Eleven, One showed up with donut holes, then there were seven.
pdl.
afro puffs
Seven little ~~angels~~ doing tricks on in-line skates, One spun into a back flip, then there were eight;
pdl.
afro puffs
Eight little ~~angels~~ in the arcade ticket line, One had golden vouchers, then there were nine.
pdl.
afro puffs
Nine little ~~angels~~ sitting up straight like gentlemen, “Is there room for me?” one cried, then there were ten!
pdl.
afro puffs
Ten little ~~angels~~ building fortresses in the snow, Then heading in to warm their toes and sneak some cookie dough.
pdl.
afro puffs
Ten little ~~angels~~ blowing bubbles in the breeze, Naming caterpillars, lady bugs, and bumble bees.
pdl.

6

ANIMATO.
Lady bugs, & bumble bees. Snips and snails and puppy dog tails, Let's count them 1 - 10;
Hammers and nails and sloops and sails, Let's count them all again!
*

ROBERTO HARRISON

email personas

what is that body of yours? a contaminate network of paradise unfolds

node i
multiplicative, subtractive IFF

and the soil of a shrine, illuminated war
by a welcome void to attend
an interior recall of the Ocean garb, as they
are a Pushing hope of color
stood under
by solid gates, no face or the gesture rains before vulnerability
a count beside fumes as penetrations report, smile—unwanted alien
for each arrow. up
as they are the dust
projected for solution, material,
light to receive a doe and her fawn, as she as he attends
a forest
of the indeterminate. and Then by the day

the winds of light escape
from the solar plexus
with each Send, never to heal
as there is nothing to receive in response. can we fit
the multi-verse
through two bits of light? all conversation
does not report what a world
will feel like for bodies . . . those, most shelters
in the Northwest Territory, 1790 (-2036, AND-THEN . . .)
Andes
ally themselves to the Battle of the Pumpkin Fields and Return

Neshoba County

not all One, none of us, the other gaze

- ” [they] appropriated the power of their enemies
  by mimicking their symbols and behavior, a process
  called mimesis.”

+ alter altar Mimesis and Alterity   Mola

Day   } “All the news . . .”   < ser, te veo ser
                                                    Bocas…

∞
achukma

Manitoba

“De noche la puerta quedaba casi abierta.”

to a wandering scar. I of that intermediate region
where the fish retain
their underwater shimmering   beside the Source of all
networks, tied turban
in the night, as she was us and is

to deport food and recover. que no
me vees, que somos juntos con los
de abajo, caminando
despues de la lluvia, escribiendo los nombres
de los diablos dentro de manos
sin piel. y cuando ellos
se notan que no somos
los olvidados y que no tenemos ojos, we
circumscribe our derailments in the West

of those who seem to stand beside the notice of the ether. our lives
cannot fulfill
you
in desperation, we cannot meet the goals
of your sewage
accomplishments, mister and missus intelligentsia, er, we
have no body to share
with your gut. what is the frazzle for? I
as she unwinds the detriment

toward the back, accounted for the science
of becoming and stood for the Net.
no more
realizations of the social intention
beyond institutional garb, they display
their homelessness
of the altered persona, faltering drives
and seasonal belonging
outside of the penetrant and the few crumbs
that align themselves with each solar
wind, with the papers
subsumed under the appearance of the neutral, and the in
between selves
that share the word electronically. Panamá,
all liminal space in all
worlds contemporaneous, how
those eyes are out of sync
with the balance of belonging
in each. what language do you share, what
world divides you to intend to others
the service
of the disappeared? where
is your face, that your body
becomes me?

Nittak

La Pietá "Sono un uomo ferito." àHugo Spadafora

not me
not i
node i

"Protection from power/phone . . ."

Oppiano

light
and more darkness

si no
si no
si no
si no

net Sun

LILY HOANG AND CARMEN GIMÉNEZ SMITH

from *Hummeltopia*

Hummel #3128: Mary Ingalls Hummel
Height: 2.07"

Mary's copper bangs are bobbypinned straight back, an imitation of her hairstyle from the television series. Her saddle shoes leave tracks of mud. With her left hand, she drags a small stack of belted topographic books. A walking stick is an extension of her right hand, natural. She is wearing a delicate peach dress, color no longer matters to her, an abstraction, more imagination than memory.

Hummel #708120: Lethal Ray Hummel
Height: 3.2 inches

A tousled blonde is crouched in a field of daisies, which are mostly painted on to the figure's pedestal.

One rosy knee bears the bright red stain of a fall. The black and red dirndl is adorned with tiny red anarchy symbols.

She's been to other wars. One was across, it seemed, a wall of vines set on its back. Brambles in everyone. Another was smoke-filled and everyone became bats.

All around her: the echo of pluck breaking open. A cushion of that sound surrounds the figurine, so it's hard to hold her without wanting to let go.

Inside her head is a scene: teeny tiny airplanes swarm her dead father's head nestled in a crown of daisies. He taught her revolt.

His private diary had recipes for word bombs and poetry missiles.

Hummel #3192013: PTSD Hummel
Height: 0.4"

A mass in fetal position, desert camouflaged. His hands form a shelter over the head. Beside him: one Dragunov Sniper Rifle, one Colt M1911, two bottles of water, one Bible, King James, a crumpled blanket.

CATHY PARK HONG

Trouble in Mind

A heartvein throbs between her brows: Ketty-San's
incensed another joke's made at her expense,

With characters of granite schist, she hashtags a ban
on all such jokes, then they, her so-
called friends, pipe up: Why are *you*
making such a stink
on race?
You're so post, you're Silicon.

Scuttle back to her spot as sidekick chum.
Her lyric's needed when they need a backup
minor key,
to that lead's blues that got no core
(*what* a snore).

But what core is Ketty-San, sidekick chum?
Torn like tendrils of bloody tenderloin
floating in the sea, heart
a stage set
about to be struck—

All nightlong, she scribbles her useless Esoterica.
All daylong, mumble-cored, she meeps,
meeps along.

"TITLE! JILLWRITES CURATES MAPS!"

Written within the festival of Lupercalia. Also, Valentine's Day. Do whatever needs to be done with it: all the things.

TITLE! JILLWRITES CURATES MAPS!
TITLE_JILLWRITES_CURATES_MAPS
Generative Excerpt From A Continuingly Evolving Memoir In Many Media
A Visual-Chronolinear Map of My Studio
Map of A Guided Tour of The Museum of JillWrites: What To See In Four Pages

[photos]
[aphorisms]
The Internet Is A Mythological Field. My Web Presence: A Tarot Deck for the Misbegotten
my grey matter I experience a dramatic situation. #postpostmodernmindtheater
PLEASE, if your car IS, or even resembles a DeLorean, DO accelerate. "Look, I went to the internet and I am alive, Neo. But I went to Derrida and I come out crying every day."
I go through excessive self-conflict to tell you about the lack of something.
Because telling you in words about a lack just isn't as true as letting it lack.
"Now is a summery discontent." –JillWrites "Now is a summary discontent." –JillWrites
Missing something? No words for you, JillWrites!

IT IS ART THAT I AM ON TWITTER AT ALL. IT IS ART THAT WE PERFORM THAT WE ARE 'NOT TALKING TO EACH OTHER'. IT IS ART THAT YOU MIGHT THINK WE DON'T KNOW EACH OTHER. IT IS ART THAT CHANDELIERS FALL.

BY MY CALCULATIONS, THE 'IMAGINATION' ITSELF IS ART. THE IDEA OF THE HUMAN IMAGINATION IS ART. EVERYTHING IS IN REAL TIME WITH OTHER HUMANS. THAT INCLUDES MEMORY. WHEN YOU ARE LOST IN MEMORY, YOU ARE IN FACT, STILL IN THE NOW WITH OTHER HUMAN BODIES. WHEN YOU ARE LOST IN IMAGINATION. YOU ARE, IN FACT, STILL IN THE NOW WITH OTHER HUMAN BODIES. WHEN YOU ARE READING. WHEN YOU ARE KISSED.
YES, SORRY, FUCKING, TOO. DON'T LET ANYONE ELSE CONTROL WHEN YOU GO TO THE BATHROOM. 'WHEN YOU HAVE TO GO, YOU HAVE TO GO.'
THE WOMAN'S URINARY TRACT IS STILL TOO CLOSE TO THE VAGINA. EVOLUTION WANTS TO FIX IT.

The presence of an explanation wouldn't convey "missing"! That's the point—it's all negative space. / The point of what? / My sculpture. / That's air. / Exactly!

What people call fate when they look at it through hindsight is in actuality the result of proactive moving-forward by the web of human necessity to move ourselves forward together. "Sure, I'd love to write a dissertation on the ethics of prophecy!" . . . is going to be heard much more often now that the Harry Potter series has spawned a generation of dark-magic-warring witches. *The whole internet is Tom Riddle's diary.*

THE WHOLE INTERNET IS TOM RIDDLE'S DIARY. THE WHOLE INTERNET IS MY/OUR/YOUR MARAUDER'S MAP.

Rereading Immanuel Kant's "An Answer to the Question: What Is Enlightenment?" He used a lot more !'s than I remembered! Or expected! It reads like a self-aware futuristic magazine text! He's very air-quotesey! But here, I agree! "Sapere aude"!

I have not written memoir. (?) I have not photo-narrated a map of my studio. (?) I have not (designed / supplied) a guided tour of my work. (?)

"I wasn't expecting myself to go straight to the MoMA, but I did think I'd . . . write a paragraph." #attentionspananarchyinthedigitalage
#JillWritesisms I've been developing my own dictionary, as I'm sure many of you are. Jillwritesism: "Whattingtheup." It's a hypothetical salutation. Please @JillWrites me on Twitter if you read this.
SUPERJillBatWomanHulkPhilosophyPhDCandidate: To become the world's foremost authority on the bio-social significance of Twitter?

I LOVE (translate: I'm somewhat embittered) that the derivative of what we've been taught about the Modernist writers amounts to they were big geniuses who knew what they were doing all along. Um. Bullshit.

Imagined Conversation Between Virginia Woolf & James Joyce, Traversing Space & Time

Soundtrack: the end of "The World Spins Madly On" (The Weepies).
JAMES JOYCE: *(Eagerly & conspiratorially, into his mirror.)* Hey, Virginia! What are you doing June 16th! (AS IF she could actually show up in Dublin, because really it would be great if really she could get there, really!)
VIRGINIA WOOLF: *(Flitting around in her Room. As if in a feathery bird-winged ballerina costume)*
(I must have deleted these Tweets. Did save the punchline? I remember this day.)

THE END

Memory! And Proust! Next: On JillWrites.

A Thoughtful Interlude With JillWrites

SHAM OVER

JILLWRITES: What happens next? Do I put on my Balenciaga gown? *(Addressing the Dickens' Miss Havisham, in absentia)* Huh, Havisham?

(A BRECHTIAN PROJECTION TITLE APPEARS ABOVE HER HEAD . . .
I MEAN . . . HERE:
HAVE! A SHAM! JUST SO YOU KNOW.)

JILLWRITES: "Have! A sham!" is how it should be pronounced. Have. A. Sham. Just so you know.

N.B. We are now having. a sham. Also: chandeliers fall. Helicopters arrive. comedy ensues JillWrites lives an entire memoir, Forrest Gumpianly. The soundtrack to Saturday Night Fever *plays the entire time. In the background. On air. Sometimes, when you cannot hear it. When the frequencies zoned out, that's when we danced* for you . . . This sh*t gets very, very absurd . . .*

The Road of Trials. *(unto / ad) ± vocabularium!* *[insert quadratic formula here]*

SHAM OVER

(A dude theatrically scurries in, no choice about it.)
SHAM OVER: Hi. I am a man. I speak.
JILLWRITES: APPARENTLY, "Sham Over" speaks. He is a real man. We have to let him think he's a character here, so we can let JillWrites be a writer. JillWrites is a writer. Sham Over is a visiting character. . . . With a flower in his mouth. He is accompanied by . . . five other characters. . . . And he speaks . . . Italian.

Years have passed. Jill and Sham are now in the tragicomedy stocks. Ros & Guil are in the stocks nearby. Jill lectures all on the male / female romcom cum BFF duo. All are enraged & alarmed. JillWrites has taken over where Nora Ephron has left off. We are all pleased. Snorri Sturleson takes over, it's really creepy and he doesn't know punctuation at all and also tone and also biology and also he never read Zen and the ARt of MotORCCYCLe Maintenance Special OPS of jillwritesia needs to be enlisted. No one here knows their rights. and they all need to be trained.

A TYPING VOICE: *CALL ME FROM THE BRIDGE OF KHAZAD-DÛM, NEA.*
JILLWRITES: *(TYPING)* *SOMEONENEEDSTODETHRONETHISGUY$$$$$$$$$ (PERFORMING:)* BUT WHERE TO PUT THE HASHTAG?!?! *(Aside)* I've got to pull the curtain on this shit.

Rehang chandelier. Repeat. Next up: Duck Tape. I could go on like this all night. But the question is: what will happen when the magic deadline arrives and I have to send this to an anthology? Do I start writing the clock in now? . . . Well, obviously. CLOCK. MANY CLOCKS. TOTO, TOO. AM I WRITING AICE IN WORDERLAND YET? YES, I THINK I AM. I'M YOUR FAIRY GODMOTHER! THE FAIRY GODMOTHER CHARACTER, ON THE FLIP SIDE, IS THE EVIL STEPMOTHER. IF JUNG WAS ALIVE, I'D HAVE TO TAKE HIM FOR A PINOT GRIGIO IN SOHO OR THE WEST LOOP. ←-- this is / "Not Me".

this is / "Not Me" / 'Tis I
cats
OKCUPID!

CATS.
BEAD.
BEACH.
WORK.
TIME.

I haven't yet found the right wherewithal to encapsulate the tone of comedy I would like to choose with you, Nerd-Reader. It seems that I keep getting kidnapped by werewolves, comedians, and Taxi Drivers. Before I can get to what you and I have in common. Which is: "books, because I like them".

Comedians are hiding in this methodological field. They're making me mimesis this. Is mimesis a verb yet? Not yet, on the official, but 'usage dictates meaning' and we're all so in the know about being sick of ourselves since the millennium at least, that I'm going to make a case to using mimesis as a verb. Why the hell not. The internet has already turned my beloved self-portraiture into the Word of the Year, "Selfie". And HAD already BEEN using "because" as a preposition because teaching kids to write essays: college writing instructors have to bond somehow because otherwise it's just us improvising 75-minute stand-up comedy routines for 30 kids at a time. Repeatedly. All week. I didn't grade your papers yet because drowning. Okay, why don't we watch a film now.

N.B.: "Film Is Literature, Too."

And now a word from our sponsor: The Internet. The Whole Internet.

good night

AISHA SASHA JOHN

I didn't want to go so I didn't go.

I did want to post something online so I posted something.
I wanted to conceal and confuse so I did.
I wanted to cover and also to reveal and so I did.
I do believe
this is a beginning.

If you sift
and then gather the dirt into a line, you have a story.
You can put perfume on that line but I'm not
anymore a liar.
I want to smell the armpits of the line
like how the unit of a poem
is your mouth.

The end.

I just wanted to say
there's no salvation here.

Just a gap
between what I am and what it was
thought I am
it
wasn't understood
and now I understand
that it wasn't understood
and I'm lonely.

Book—you're no more a friend than my thighs.

And I have all these conversations with various yous
and in them I explicate my position
and cement it really
which is not—
it's not grace.

And I don't want to
talk about my plans my intentions my plans or
hold up my plans to any scrutiny or better them or
read up about you more
to try to learn your choreography like
as if I am not so subtle elegant and of grace as I am now
in this bold blue sweater of my 2nd best friend
as the caffeine energizes my spectrum
and the colour of the sky slaps me in a sexual way.
I think about the whole length of the day
and where in it I can inject a joy deep into its tissue.

Do you tire of me?
Should I abandon you?
Am I holding too
closely unto your neck?
Have I been a
greedy one and
noisy?
Have I been very noisy
and you suffer in a
quiet way with
secret
and I have suffered also too in this way maybe
grace is to let our suffering
take a walk
and be seen with all its regions showing.
My flat ass
and
beautiful decisions
are calling me.
Are you going to call me?
I
can do everything today.
If I wear the loveliest tights from Winners
I can bike and never be killed.
I can prompt
the sacking of oppressors
and not be
revenged upon,
have a high fat snack and then
soar as
is my duty.

I never thought—and I don't care I just never
thought, "Toronto."
Never.

I can tell you
anything.
As I hold up my blouse
and show you
my world.
I can give you everything
and together we'll advance
for the hot hope of you
getting actual
and me
getting actual too.

I'm sleepy.

“Purple in her womb or
dark in her bosom or
dark in her lap
or
violets in her bosom”

I guess I just
wanted to
come here.
Yeah.
I wanted to come here—
because
it is nice here.

I wanted to tell you some secrets.
I want a different relationship to my stories.
I said I am cold and tired of where I have been as a supplicant
when I am here and north and bourgeois, they'll eat a
better dinner than I will eat but
I also will tonight in my sweet dress, my eyeballs filled with roses,
dance.
I will dance.

And in this way I am extending
and I'm not interested in comparison because I can basically
not give a shit I mean I've got five, six senses and then there's
the whole blue universe
like
the sound of a hard crust collapsing
the baguette as it's torn
it and the other noises that have
wet my ear lately the
tinkle
the violet tinkle of the nail spa alarm system
and the hard and unhopeful scrapes of their chairs
my sisters, my brothers, of the food court
the ignoble scrape of the metal would
ruin me except
I can't be ruined.

What time is it? 137

I hope you come here with your rented car.

You're not coming.
And I can't have you this evening.
I have to put the flowers around my
own throat.
And buy myself a film.
The plush seats
will be the violets of my lap.
I'm going to begin now
anointing myself with the oil of
your absence. That is this book.
And I made the book of you
in your absence
and I'll come into the house
and in the hot oil of your absence
my anointment
is a rose-shaped burn
at my crown.
I'll buy me flowers and cover my chest
protecting my health in violets. I can't stop.
But I can have this open
and we might
communion then
right among the spaces
between
my side and arm and your
arm and side
and your thick
torso
and behind that your
tight heart
and the space between that nut and
some energy around which there is no space.
We dip dates into a good wine

and have communion.
Have we the same
mouth?

Sometimes.

BLAIR JOHNSON

The overlap of three translations of Kafka's "Imperial Message"[1]

The Emperor sent a message from his death bed to you subject shadow the imperial sun. He the kneel bed and whispered the message. It that he it. He confirmed head. Of his death all obstructing walls have been down and the great of empire in a all he. The messenger a man. Arm he through the. He resistance, he points to his breast of the sun. But the so. If open how he would fly and soon you hear his fist on your door. But instead how. He is still his way through the of the innermost palace. Never will he. And nothing would. He fight his way down the and he nothing would. He would have to the and after the and and a palace and so on thousands of years. And if he burst through the outermost but can never never happen the capital the of the world him sediment. Through here with a message from dead. You sit at your window and dream when evening.

[1] Formed by preserving only the words that had been translated identically in each version (and removing all divergent translations). The three translations used are by Ian Johnston, Willa and Edwin Muir, and Mark Harman.

I consider writing (a love poem)

I consider writing (a love poem)	I think	in the unattainable	pinned like moth bodies	somewhere else	thoughts unflatten	heavy nervousness	I don't want you to die
I'm stopped at a plateau	yes	yes	no	no	yes	yes	yes
the wrong word	yes	no	no	no	yes	yes	yes
already unreachable	yes	yes	no	yes	yes	yes	yes
try to talk	yes	no	no	no	no	no	yes
I have, I am	yes	yes	no	yes	yes	yes	yes
a problem with things	yes	yes	yes	no	no	yes	yes
never staying still	yes	yes	no	yes	yes	yes	yes
what could I have	no	yes	no	yes	yes	yes	yes
written down	no	no	no	no	no	no	yes
I make small captures	yes	yes	yes	yes	yes	yes	yes
instead	yes	no	yes	yes	yes	no	yes
I spit out vast words	no	yes	no	no	no	yes	yes
it's all gone	no	yes	yes	no	no	no	yes
it will eat everything	yes	yes	yes	yes	yes	yes	yes
it will swallow space	yes	yes	yes	yes	yes	yes	yes
none of these feel right	no	no	no	no	no	no	yes
you have your reasons	yes	yes	yes	yes	no	yes	yes
when unnameable	yes	yes	yes	no	yes	yes	yes
what is it changing	yes	no	no	yes	yes	yes	yes
I don't want you to die	yes	yes	yes	yes	yes	yes	yes

JANINE JOSEPH

Between Chou and the Butterfly

I.

On my way to America I am in an airplane

On a boat When my life is a story I am a good
swimmer An American Dream A guest
worker Freeloader Fence-hopper Uninsured brother
carried from hospital to hospital A *crushing*
caseload A *wrenching anecdote* A *deserving*
young people An anchor

II.

Before anyone finds me I am heartwood exposed
by lightning By the Young Republicans
By newscasters playing Find the Illegal Immigrant
Find the unwed single The crier The spouse
battered by a U.S. citizen spouse Find the *widow(er)*
The one you will *petition* to marry The *headless*
bodies in the Arizona desert they found

III.

I hear they raid when you're naked
in bed Packed like a sardine Pillows tucked
around you I hear Like dogs Like *Alien Relatives*
While you cry and hug They swarm
They ax your back door

IV.

The trunks of trees They ax
the wild terrain The scrub The rapid
succession of sounds I make
when I walk alone And sweaty And hardly
myself in the dark where a man
Migrating *Suffering great pain* Is found
hanging from a tree later charred

V.

According to eyewitnesses
I am the same *crazy* lost on my way
to the *Deadman's Tree* To the hollowed *Tree*
of the Virgin In the *Valley of the Lost Ones*
In the wilderness Stripped of my underwear
For the money stitched into the seams
For a mental status evaluation A physical examination
(to include complete disrobing)

VI.

Worse than *genital herpes* The situation
with these *illegals*
Into the microphone Says the interviewee

VII.

I, the undersigned
Am not a *Communist* Am not *likely to become*
a public charge I understand I do not
traffic other humans *Recruit child soldiers*
I do not seek to *practice polygamy Engage*
in espionage In *ordered genocide* In items A–L

I do not have to reimburse *the school* I do *solemnly swear*
if I am not who I say I am I *may subject me*
to permanent exclusion

BHANU KAPIL

Monster Checklist

MONSTER CHECKLIST: Syllabus Notes for The Hybrid: Spring 2014 (The Jack Kerouac School of Disembodied Poetics)

MONSTER CHECKLIST: [I have made your checklist extreme. To compensate. To give you more than you need. To deliver an excess. See: early statements, via Elizabeth Grosz, on art-making and the trait.]

[Have your sequence next to your notebook and journal in response to these questions. Your answers might also propagate material that could be returned to your essay]:

1. State the design goal for your collected work thus far: implicit here are both your intentions and your failures.

2. What kind of paper do you want to print your work on? [Larissa Lai]

3. What is happening with the body in your writing? What is happening as kinship/cross-touch/exchange/transfer between "animal, vegetal and digital" [Lai] domains?

4. How does [do] the body or bodies in your sequence move through a larger social space or territory? What is the crisis of this larger space?

5. As you did when you were a reader, create a "live narration" [Jen Hofer] no longer than a paragraph, of your sequence thus far. This could be a list of gestures or radiant nodes tracked by your own readers, or a combination of what you also—are startled/delighted by in your own work. Or: this could be a radical translation of some kind.

6. Can you bring the internal spaces of vital [bodily] life—the work with movement, gesture, membranes—to the space/matter of transitions between pieces or within the sequence.

IDEAS:

Soft tissue that is scarred is abraded/healed through XFF. Cross fiber friction. Can you create a diagonal cut or mark/erasure at the end of one piece and the beginning of the next?

Thinking about Juliana Spahr's individual/communal progression during the symposium. Is the space between texts a place to open to the communal? How? With a question? With an attention to the materials of construction? Direct address? Look back through class findings to cull strategies. Pronouns. An ethics. A tracking of the social space of [4].

Via *Nilling*, which was there one day. In the class shrine. Create a more folded environment at the thresholds of pieces. Beginnings and endings. Or of the frame as a whole. How? Last week and the week before, we spoke about atomization, figuration, slowed down or variegated time. Repetition. Again, see: class findings. And why is the fold visceral? Because it is both peristaltic and absorptive. It is polyrhythmic. See: the intestinal tract. Or the surfaces of alleyway walls in Cairo.

Place pressure on the sequence. How? Is there a body? A character? Introduce a new body [figure]. The potential for encounter. Or have what [who] is already in the sequence—as body or narrator or I or not I—reach out: and touch. Something. Initiate the spectrum of agency: relation, oppression, desire. . . .

7. "Do you feel love for your design?"—David, undergraduate student, architecture program, Pratt Institute.

8. "Perhaps specificities and endpoints are not what we need." Larissa Lai. Can you make an aesthetic statement about your engagement with the vital forms of our class: monster, hybrid, assemblage, gesture and so on. How did the category, Hybrid, generate a restless feeling in you? I am trying to ask you to address the emotion you have or do not have about the activity of having revised your sequence. What unfolded for you, both in germinal ways and also this last part of the process, when the thing begins to move or falls apart on its own bones? What do you know about the culture and sociality underlying your work? Your drive to imagine? Your connection to another world?

9. What is the dream of your work? What is being imagined? Write: an aesthetics of the future that is rooted in your own creative practice for this class. [See: Larissa Lai's class handout for The Insurgent Architect Dreams the Future, if you attended her class last week.]

10. What is the place of the fragment in your work? What sensations accompany the fragment or are propagated by it?

11. What will you carry with you?

12. What will you leave behind?

13. Assess the biopolitics of your piece. What forms of cosmic and earthly contact or expression are happening in your piece? This is a question about incubation: the capacity of a text to mutate. This is a question about what nourishes your monster or wakes it up. How will you make the lightning bolt strike the tulip?

14. How did you fail?

RUTH ELLEN KOCHER

Insomnia Cycle 44

She' s the queen of Neo-Soul   Slow it down   Heya   Suddenly I'm standing   What do you want from me   You make me want to leave   Look   It's not about music   There were three young orphans   Four   But about that   Make it disappear   The truth will vanish with them   The truth has your word   The truth is almost   Hey, stupid   Don't be so dramatic   They make fortunes building bombs   The stone age is before us   Get outta here   Go on   The story won't get out   It's not about music   It's not about making something that makes something else   She snaps her fingers but the earth quakes   She *ah   ah   ahhhhs* but He still came home   She sways a dance we don't know how to name   When you want your horizon to work, you'll celebrate it first   There were four orphans but you don't remember their names   Suddenly, they're gone   You don't have to pay a cent   Put that money in your pocket   She sings for free   She knows that Truth is ancient and extinct   She knows there are things that can change you forever   In the darkest times, the canyon is unexpected and still there   The canyon is in her belly and full of C notes   The canyon is an assailant   The story won't get out   The truth refuses to name a source   Slow it down   No one talks about the truth anymore   Suddenly, I'm standing   Goodbye   Don't come back

AARON KUNIN

from "An Essay on Tickling"

Out of the body I wander
And communicate with other
Bodies, in "the" ordinary
Way "of" doing
Things, says "the" soul. But my freedom
Consists mainly

"In" "my" body's immediate
Response to "my" intentions. Pain
Sex "and" laughter imprison me
"In my" "body."
"I" can give myself "pain," "I can"
Get "myself" off;

Laughing, "my body" holds "me" so
That "I" can't tickle "myself." One
Stage is a kind "of" playing where
I'm hovering
Between pretending "to" react
"And" "pretending"

Not "to react." Holding "myself"
Together, almost "in" love "with"
"The" surrender "my" composure
Averts. That's when
"I" completely lose it, helpless
"In" disarray

"My" lost "composure" inciting
More "laughter." "One" moment like "that"
Leads "to" another, increasing
"Like" "a" laddered
Stocking: "The" first tear widens "with"
Each new attack.

There's "a" last "stage" on "the" "other"
Side "of" losing "composure" "where"
"My body" has nothing "to" "give"
"And" tries "to" laugh.
This "stage" "is" "mainly" exhaustion
"And" emptiness

"And" some "pain." "The" discovery
"Of" "laughter" must have been tickling
"The" sense "of" humor came later.
Notice "the" strange
Reversal "when" your deadpan fails
You "lose" "your" grip

While "you" "laugh" at "your" own antics
"Your" listeners do "not" "laugh." It's
Exactly "like" being tickled.
Frigidity
"And" diminished responsiveness
("One" step closer

"To" having no "sense of humor")
"To" "the" sensation "of" "being
Tickled" are two symptoms "of" "one"
Variety
"Of" impotence. Example "of"
Dualism.

DAVID LAU

In the Lower World's Tiniest Grains

There was, I was try . . .
the Burkeanism of that guy,
the Tennis-Court-Oathification stripe of a leopard sky.

"The fruit that exists in every way is a kind of sandal.
Refulgent with afters wildly reaching is open."

And they fought very hard
to kill (plural)
people in Khost with Dark Star,
the LA variety.
These guys stick maneuver

on you
("That's what we do.")

Line shatters dealings, virtues,
traders, treasures, comers, buyers, lovers,
mergers, justice, court, balance, weight—

the seal absorbs us.

from *I RL, YOU RL*

I DON'T
WANT
ANYTHING
TO DO
WITH THE
INTERNET

i mean //

homie.

you think
youre chill?

x_x

HAH
#fsho.

hold up dogg

youre like
an orange cone

im suppose to hit
in ONE-SHOT!

welcome to my couch
u superficial motherfucka

where I Smoke
in my kimono

and tweet about you

#lol

LooK:

Draper found my 20 dollars . . .

it was “blackout
tuesday”
5am a

pile of vom
casting a fort

on the street.
i really wanted

a good day off . . .
with a makeup bag

on the F train
getting proposed to twice

and finally
Nothing.

oh my god yes
oh my godwhat

in the anecdotes
and parables
composed
of former future
I found a piece
that made me
largely Rethink the
garden

as a screensaver
DEEPLY structured
to alienate

the

world.

read it.

who wants to be

in a kiss-ass

little

novel?
I do.

I'd be willing

to deface
a polygamous

promise a
liberal

Lil'
homeboy .

Shot in the dark:
Lately I find

an entertaining
interest in

Salman Rushdie,
OG Man of Insight

coolest dude
in the name of

our bigot "hemisphere".
Santorum won

the general election.
our heads
were shat on.

All of them.

@Lord:
talk me out of

“dicks” tonight.

rite now

i’m “that girl”
the one

googling screenshot
#art and meaning.

i just wanna
cast sum spells
to remember

u in europe u
20 years old
and Every time

it’s 3 am i
just want a jack
could u be

the jack
to my liz
lemon?

I'M not like scared
of you but 3% of my HEAD is in
"Actual pain."

Everything I feel is
sweaty & hot
like an early evening

movie or like fucking
in the middle

of a summer city day.

Motherfucker, you

#CONTRADICTION

heat, you Hot child
STOP making me
nervous. Everything I like
is 97% wrong.

WHEN can I love you
                & have it feel
                                right.

http://i am
a Facebook
profile.

the imminent
up and coming
underground.

http://bulk
literature.com/
just-wondering.

woof . . . the beast

announcement. he
is a magazine

sensation. i-have-
come-out-of-july-
days—my thoughts

as new as deli
meat. http://
. . . owell

SUEYEUN JULIETTE LEE

[G calls]

from *Juliette and the Boys*

G calls
the Dutchman arrived
he's had
a hundred swords
hanging over him
$40K
files 17th century
paperclips keeps
the stoned mannequin
upright
in the basement
thinks about me
now
at lunch
in the morning, too
at night with
trains outside
will I on the phone
with his mom all
breathless next time
it hurts
it rings on
Friday, yes yes

AMY LORRAINE LONG

Product Warning

PATIENT PRESCRIPTION INFORMATION

McCowen, Ryan 12/16/02
1700 18th Street
Niceville, FL 32578
Ph: 850.533-0592 Refills: 0

METHADONE 10 MG TABLETS
TAKE 1 TABLET BY MOUTH TWICE DAILY

This is a WHITE, OVAL-shaped TABLET imprinted with 54 142 on the front.
METHADONE – ORAL – (METH a done)

USES: I didn't ask Ryan why he had methadone pills when he'd told me that a nurse watched him drink his methadone at the clinic every morning. I didn't know yet that Ryan bought or had doctors prescribe him extra opiates because the clinic dose didn't get him high. And despite what he said, Ryan really just wanted to get high. I guess it occurred to me, and I guess I didn't care. I had never been high, and I'd never wanted to get high. People ask what drew me to Ryan back then or what compelled me to take methadone when I'd never even been stoned. I can't answer them. Except maybe to say that Ryan was twenty-two and looked like a cross between Conor Oberst and Kurt Cobain and that my ability—at eighteen—to say I'd never been high made me sound silly and young and boring when I heard the words in his ears.
HOW TO USE: I should have been scared, but I wasn't. I don't know why. Probably an OVAL-shaped, WHITE TABLET felt safe. A pharmacist in a clean white jacket dispenses OVAL-shaped, WHITE TABLETS; a doctor prescribes them. Ryan removed three OVAL-shaped, WHITE TABLETS from a translucent orange bottle with his name on it. His name on that bottle sanctioned the pills. He gave one to me and took two for himself.

SIDE EFFECTS: I swallowed my pill and twenty minutes later emerged as a pool of warm, scratchy light. When I talked, I knew I had a right to what I said. I don't remember what I said. What I said didn't matter. It only mattered that I said it, that I wasn't the girl who'd sat mute and dumb when Ryan propped his feet up on my dash that first day and told me all about his heroin addiction and his dead girlfriend and his move back to Destin from New York City. I didn't feel self-conscious and awkward the way I'd felt around Ryan when I could say I'd never been high. High, I felt electric. I felt brilliant. I felt like a badass. But I can't say that I took methadone because I wanted to feel like an electric, brilliant badass. I didn't know how opiates would make me feel until I took one; I don't think I'd even considered it. I think I started doing drugs because I wanted a boy to like me.

DRUG INTERACTIONS: We took the methadone, and then Ryan and I snorted cocaine he cut into lines on a desk in the half-finished apartment above his dad's auto shop, where he lived when I first knew him. I don't remember wondering why we were doing cocaine when Ryan had told me three days earlier that he wanted to get clean. Post-cocaine, my memory splices a few individual frames into an otherwise blank reel. I remember lying with Ryan on the floor, neck bent so my chin stuck in the air; he said the coke would hit harder if I let it drip straight into my throat. I remember tracing with my index finger the skull-and-crossbones tattoo on his wrist, but that might have been another time. Mostly, I remember standing in Walmart cashing a check so we could buy more coke. I don't remember how I felt the first time I did cocaine, but I know because I wrote the check that I wanted to feel it more.

OVERDOSE: One-hundred pound girls shouldn't take drugs from basically strange men. But opiated and coked up, I felt safe because I'd been careless. I mimicked Ryan's cocky saunter and decided I would be, should be, maybe always had been someone else. Someone else might have been smarter about mixing opiates with amphetamines; I had no tolerance at all, and adding an upper to a downer put stress on my unsuspecting heart. But that night Ryan didn't feel like a stranger, and I didn't know about tolerances and bad chemical combinations, so I couldn't die.

PATIENT PRESCRIPTION INFORMATION

McCowen, Ryan 01/13/03
700 18th St.
Niceville, FL 32601 Refills: 1 before 01/13/04
Ph: 850.533-0592

ALPRAZOLAM 2 MG TABLETS
TAKE 1 CAPSULES BY MOUTH THREE TIMES DAILY

This is a WHITE, OBLONG-shaped, MULTI-SCORED TABLET imprinted with R039 on the front.

ALPRAZOLAM – ORAL – (al PRAY zoe lam)
COMMON BRAND NAME(S): Xanax

USES: When I asked him how it would feel, Ryan said Xanax would relax me. He started taking it for panic attacks, which is the only true thing I ever heard him tell a doctor. But he took it so often—just to relax, just because he could—that when panic struck his heart wouldn't stop racing and his palm wouldn't stop throbbing unless he took three or four times his prescribed dose. I'd never had a panic attack, but I believed or maybe agreed with Ryan when he said I needed to relax.
HOW TO USE: On our first date, Ryan crushed up a Xanax bar with his ID and a cassette-tape case on the center console of my 1997 Chrysler Intrepid. He divided the powder into two lines and sniffed one up his nose through a rolled-up dollar bill. I thought the Xanax would be sticky like the coke, so I inhaled too hard. I coughed and held my thumb to my burning nostril in case all the powder spewed out when I also exhaled too hard.
SIDE EFFECTS: Touching my own hair felt like petting an expensive stuffed toy, light and pillowy. We walked down the block hand-in-hand, and our skin was like worn-in cotton. We saw a movie called *Narc*. *Narc* opened in late 2002 and did so poorly at the box office that it released straight to the cheap second-run theater where Ryan and I saw it. I have no memory of the movie at all except that the scenes were dark and the plot had something to do with

the DEA. I kept leaning over to ask Ryan what had happened and who was who until the credits rolled without warning. "What?" I said. "That movie was, like, five minutes long." After the novelty wore off, Xanax didn't turn me plush-doll soft and disoriented; I just felt relaxed, like Ryan said I would. But we never relaxed about Xanax; if Ryan didn't have any, the withdrawal could induce seizures. He'd been on it for years.

DRUG INTERACTIONS: I used Xanax to potentiate other drugs and come down from coke. I took it after near-catastrophes, like if Ryan got ripped off by a dealer or couldn't get a new opiate prescription when he needed one (and he always needed one). Sometimes the near-catastrophe was a fight. Ryan liked to fuck with me. He told me he'd cheated on me or contracted HIV or been possessed by a demon. He threatened to tell my parents that I hadn't stopped seeing him like they'd insisted but had actually let him move with me to Gainesville, where we were right then getting high in a motel room his mother paid for. I believed everything, even his *Exorcist* impressions, until he laughed and told me he'd made it all up. Sometimes he waited until I believed that, too, and said he'd lied about lying. I'd get mad, and then I'd cry, and Ryan would console me as though he had the right. I don't know why I let him, and I don't know why I put up with it except that Ryan said he loved me, and I said I loved him, too. In love, I thought, you were supposed to cry.

OVERDOSE: Ryan would pile too much Xanax on top of too many opiates and nod out. Usually it was nothing: his head dropped, and his cigarette burned streaks into my car's upholstery or holes in our sheets and his shirts. Nod, blink, repeat. Other times he stopped breathing, and I had to shake him back to life. When I couldn't get him on the phone, I just knew he'd died. Even now, when someone doesn't answer my calls, I picture the person dead.

PATIENT PRESCRIPTION INFORMATION

Long, Amy 01/09/04
45 Springs Residential Complex
Gainesville, FL 32601 Refills: 0
Ph: 850.582-4074

HYDROCODONE-CHLORPHENIRAMINE
7.5–500/15ML SYRUP
TAKE 5ML EVERY TWELVE HOURS

This is a YELLOW SYRUP.

HYDROCODONE-CHLORPHENIRAMINE – ORAL – (KLOR fen IR a meen and HYE droe KOE done)
COMMON BRAND NAME(S): Tussionex

USES: Ryan told doctors that a car he'd been working under fell on him and pinched his sciatic nerve. He'd say he was new to town and needed someone to write his painkillers until an appointment opened up at the pain management center, where they'd run tests and take X-rays and find nothing wrong with his back. I didn't need a story. I actually exhibited the symptoms for which Tussionex is indicated: nasal congestion, sore throat, body aches, a cough so savage it left my ribs sore. "Last time I had this, my doctor gave me . . . I think it was called Tussionex?" I said like someone who couldn't recite the periodic table of opiates off the top of her head. I found Ryan in the parking lot and waved the prescription over my head like a captured flag.
HOW TO USE: We passed the amber plastic bottle back and forth as I drove to our room at the Gainesville Lodge. Ryan unlocked the door and lit a cigarette. I'd cut back to preserve my throat, but I had a fresh opiate buzz and sugary Tussionex coating my tongue, so I took one, too, and curled up under the never-washed blanket I knew I shouldn't use. Even on Tussionex I didn't feel like getting out of bed, but Ryan had friends in town and wanted to take them out that night. "Don't make me look like a jackass," he said and said until I walked downtown with them anyway. When the bouncer waved me off (I wasn't twenty-one), I faked disappointment and walked back alone, eager to slip out of my jeans and into stiff sheets.

SIDE EFFECTS: The bars had been closed for over an hour when Ryan stumbled drunk into our room with a girl I didn't know. He flicked on a lamp. I snapped at him to turn it off. The girl was dressed for the bar; it didn't seem fair that she should see me unwashed and ugly with a cold. "I told Tara she could use the bathroom," Ryan said, as if her full bladder rendered the rest of her body benign. I'd have described Tara as chubby, maybe because her curves made me look twelve. She was cute, though. Pert nose and anime eyes, pixie cut dyed a pinkish red. She seemed too comfortable in our room, not bothered enough that I was there. Ryan and I whispered to each other while Tara pissed, and he took too much time walking her to her car. "On your side," I said when he climbed into bed fully clothed.

DRUG INTERACTIONS: In the morning I told Ryan I'd be back in an hour. I spent it just sitting in the dorm room I never used. I returned exactly when I'd said I would and found Tara and her friend Tammy eating ninety-nine-cent burritos at the foot of our bed. Ryan said they'd dropped by, that he didn't invite them. They were both too friendly. While I kicked them out, Tara invited Ryan and me over to get stoned and play Mario Kart after. She spoke as though she didn't know what I needed to say to him. Or maybe she knew exactly and so knew, too, that her invitation already excluded me.

OVERDOSE: Ryan cursed and pleaded and painted impossible white picket fences into our future. He grabbed at threads the way he'd done once with my checkbook when I wouldn't pay $175 for a pill-mill doctor in Ocala. "I *need* you," he said. If he could make me feel guilty, I might change my mind; I'd done it before. But now I had Tara—something concrete to which I could point and say, "That." Ryan couldn't count on Tara yet. He cried. Actual tears. But I held firm. Ryan put on his shoes and asked me to drive him to Tara's house. "I could use to get stoned and play Mario Kart," he said. I kissed him for what I said would be the last time and dropped him on his new girlfriend's doorstep.

PATIENT PRESCRIPTION INFORMATION

McCowen, Ryan 03/06/04
1100 SW 8th Ave
Gainesville, FL 32601 Refills: 0
Ph: 352.718-0363

OXYCODONE HCI/APAP 5/500 MG CAPSULE
TAKE 1-2 CAPSULES BY MOUTH AS NEEDED FOR PAIN

This is a RED/WHITE, CAPSULE-shaped CAPSULE imprinted with M 392/54 392 on the side.

OXYCODONE HCI/APAP – ORAL – (OX I KOE done and a SEET a MIN oh fen)
COMMON BRAND NAME(S): Tylox

USES: Ryan went back on the methadone clinic, but Tara wouldn't drive him there. He took the bus or begged rides from me. When he could afford it, Ryan bought pills from other patients on the clinic steps. When he couldn't, he subsisted on his methadone and prescriptions from a dentist who once wrote him Percocet for some gnarly tooth infection. The third time he called to complain that his tooth still bothered him, Dr. Smiles switched Ryan from Percocet to Tylox: oxycodone cut with way too much Tylenol. The pills were weak and dirty, but Ryan did what he could with what he got.
HOW TO USE: Tara learned to use what she could get, too, except all she could get was me. I'd take Ryan to the clinic or to fill his Tylox prescriptions, then sit on his futon and watch him open RED/WHITE, CAPSULE-shaped CAPSULES, pour their powder onto his kitchenette counter, and snort piles of gold-ish granules every ten minutes because that's about how long a Tylox high lasts. I drew the line at putting five-hundred milligrams of acetaminophen up my own nose.
SIDE EFFECTS: Ryan and I got along better when we weren't dating. I remembered why I'd liked him in the first place. He was familiar. He grew up right beside me. He knew what I meant when I told stories about watching

my friends skateboard at The Landing or seeing shows in church basements after the Java Pit closed. I had heard rumors about his friends, and he'd heard rumors about mine. He talked to me in a way that no one else in Gainesville could because we had the same touchstones. He made me laugh. He gave unbeatable head. Ryan and I never had penetrative sex while we were a couple, and we didn't have it when we cheated on Tara, either. He swore he never shared needles, but I was too smart now to bet my life on what Ryan said. Besides, I'd shared all my other below-the-waist firsts with him; I wanted to experience my last first with someone new.

DRUG INTERACTIONS: Ryan winked at his penis when he wanted me to go down on him. The wink wasn't funny or sexy; it erased any desire I had to so much as approach his dick. He thought I'd change my mind if his fingers or tongue hit the right spots. But the second I felt myself about to come, I pushed him off me. "I can't do this," I'd say, and Ryan would groan as though Tara were actually my girlfriend, my problem. But the problem wasn't just Tara. I knew I was doing the wrong thing. I think I kept doing it to prove that I hadn't been rejected, that Ryan still wanted me. But I'd seen what he could offer and said I didn't want it. I'd rejected him. For two months I hovered on the verge of an orgasm I felt too guilty and too confused to achieve. Ryan hardly ever finished either, but he didn't act like it mattered much. He put on his clothes and pulled apart another Tylox.

OVERDOSE: I don't remember how Tara found out. Maybe she walked in on us. Maybe someone told her, but I don't know who could have. Probably Ryan said something. He may have wanted to make Tara jealous, or maybe it started as a joke and she saw through it. Maybe Ryan did to Tara the same thing he'd done to me, and maybe she stopped at angry and never settled into sad. I wasn't there (unless I was). The next time she saw me, Tara poured her beer on my head from the second-floor alcove at the University Club. I guess I deserved it, but I went upstairs and called her a cunt anyway. "What did you think would happen?" I asked. "He cheated on me with you."

PATIENT PRESCRIPTION INFORMATION

McCowen, Ryan 08/24/04
1700 18th St.
Gainesville, FL 32601 Refills: 0
Ph: 850.533-0592

HYDROCODONE-APAP 7.5/300MG TABLETS
TAKE 1 TABLET BY MOUTH THREE TIMES DAILY

This is a WHITE, OVAL-shaped, SCORED TABLET imprinted with M358 on the front.

HYDROCODONE-APAP – ORAL – (hye droe KOE done and a SEET a MIN oh fen)
COMMON BRAND NAME(S): Vicodin, Lortab, Norco

USES: Ryan kept trying Shands even after he'd seen "NO NARCOTICS" scrawled on his chart, and sometimes he left with a prescription. He still used the herniated disc story and the recent move excuse, even when he'd lived in Gainesville for almost a year. If a doctor noticed all his ER visits and asked why Ryan still hadn't seen a pain expert, he put his head in his hands and cited unemployment and uninsurability. You could believe it if you wanted to, and Ryan made you want to. I assume he brought Tara into the exam room with him the way he brought me. We were props, effective as his fake hobble. Because girls like us—nice girls, college girls—don't date junkies.
HOW TO USE: I only know what Ryan told me: that he'd miscalculated his pharmacy schedule and brought his prescription to a CVS he'd used two weeks earlier. Florida didn't have a narcotic registry yet, so pharmacists flagged patients they suspected of doctor shopping. CVS suspected Ryan, and one of the techs called the police. The cops interrogated Tara, and I think it scared her. I don't think she really knew what Ryan was doing. She talked about his drug use as an annoyance or an endearing quirk but not as something illegal. Maybe she thought Ryan's prescriptions were legitimate because doctors wrote them; she may not have known that he was obligated to tell each one what the others did. Either way, Tara decided that Ryan wasn't worth risking a criminal

record. She could handle infidelity, but she dumped him when he got arrested.
SIDE EFFECTS: Alachua County charged Ryan with concealing information to obtain a controlled substance and sentenced him to six months in jail. Tara wouldn't visit, so I did. We sat on steel benches and cracked barbed jokes at the other's expense into black plastic phones. Ryan laughed when other inmates hit on me. "Come see me, baby," they'd call over concrete-block partitions. I teased them, said "Next time." We made fun of Tara's innocence and pretended it had never been mine. I felt safer, less reckless with a plexiglass wall between us. I didn't worry about how Ryan would get his Xanax or stave off opiate withdrawal. And he couldn't touch me, so we couldn't fall back into old, bad patterns.
DRUG INTERACTIONS: Before she knew that Ryan and I had fucked around behind her back, Tara considered us friends. I think she felt guilty about interrupting my relationship, and I felt sorry for her, four years older than I was and with no better sense. She left beers in bathroom stalls for me to chug, and I offered up my Ryan expertise. Once she ran three blocks in the rain pursuing a stranger who asked for a ride home from the bar and then stole my passenger seat's headrest when I kicked him out of the car. But now we were enemies. When she changed her mind about making visits, Ryan and I planned mine so Tara would never know about them. The schedule got so complicated that I let her take it over. Ryan receded into my background. Tara picked him up when the county released him at midnight in February.
OVERDOSE: Tara wanted Ryan to clean up, and he kept doing the same shit. After they broke up, Ryan was at my house all the time. He came over and distracted me when I told him I needed to work. He stole weed from the container I kept perpetually stocked on my coffee table and palmed any money I left out in the open. He woke me up at six in the morning, banging on my windows like I'd already agreed to drive him to the clinic. When I told him I didn't want him in my house anymore, Ryan shoved open the door I blocked with my body and entered anyway. I wasn't strong enough to stop him, and I was too embarrassed to admit I was scared. I got tougher. I got better at saying no. But I couldn't shake the feeling that I owed him something.

PATIENT PRESCRIPTION INFORMATION

Long, Amy	11/30/06
1113 SW 4th Ave	
Gainesville, FL 32601	Refills: 0
Ph: 850.582-4074	

CLONAZEPAM 1 MG TABLETS

TAKE 1-2 BY MOUTH AS NEEDED FOR ANXIETY

This is a ROUND, WHITE, SCORED TABLET imprinted with R 34 on the front.

CLONAZEPAM - ORAL - (kloe NAZ e pam)
COMMON BRAND NAME(S): Klonopin

USES: I remember exactly the episode of *Grey's Anatomy* I was watching when my heart started racing and wouldn't stop. I knew I'd die; the muscle would give out or crack through my ribcage. I drove myself to the ER at Shands—I could see it from my house—ticking off cardiovascular disorders on my steering wheel. The nurse who did my EKG told me that, yes, this could be a heart attack. When I saw a doctor, he told me I'd had a panic attack—there was nothing actually wrong with my heart—and wrote me a prescription for a dozen Xanax.

HOW TO USE: I didn't want to take Xanax for the rest of my life; it's too short-acting and too addictive. I went to a doctor Ryan used to see and told him I'd rather take Klonopin. I didn't think of what I did as doctor shopping. I didn't think of myself as imitating Ryan. I simply knew that this doctor would write me what I asked for and wouldn't stop writing it unless I stopped asking for it.

SIDE EFFECTS: Ryan would have stolen my Klonopin, too, but by then he wasn't legally allowed within 500 feet of me. At the courthouse, I didn't know how to fill out the forms. Ryan and I weren't married or dating; he'd never physically hurt me. I said he'd tried to break into my house. I didn't say that after he did I drove him to the methadone clinic. The police took almost a week to serve Ryan with the papers, and until Ryan had seen and signed the papers, the restraining order didn't mean anything. He was never home. I didn't know where or if he worked. He knocked on my door once, sat smoking at my picnic table to see if I'd come out. He didn't know about the papers. He didn't know that if I talked to him I'd void my own restraining order. I dropped to my knees and crawled across the hardwood floors in my own home so Ryan wouldn't see me. The 911 operator didn't seem to register the urgency in my voice or understand what I meant when I whispered that I needed an officer to serve my ex with an injunction. By the time a cop ambled over holding no papers, Ryan had left.

DRUG INTERACTIONS: Once I sat right beside Ryan on my weed dealer's couch and didn't even know it until he said, "This is a lot closer than 500 feet." Ryan had buzzed his hair, packed on ten or fifteen new pounds. But his voice hadn't changed. I bolted up off my seat. "You have to leave," I said. "You can't be here." Ryan said that sounded like Jimmy's decision. Jimmy didn't want to get involved. But we all knew I wouldn't call the police. Another time Ryan had his friend Gideon call me and ask after him. Gideon and Ryan sound like twins: same nasal voice, Northwest Florida accent, heroin slur. "If I didn't know better," I said a few minutes in, "I'd swear you were Ryan." Ryan said, "I am, idiot." Gideon had passed him the phone.

OVERDOSE: I used to get sick when semesters ended. Like my body knew I couldn't afford a week in bed until I'd finished all my papers. I didn't think about my panic attacks that way until I started writing about Ryan, searching Docket 01 2006 DR 001262 on the Alachua County Clerk of Court website for dates I needed to know. I filed for the injunction in April. Gideon called in August. That episode of *Grey's Anatomy* aired on Thanksgiving, when I thought it was all over. But maybe listening for Ryan's footsteps in my yard and keeping tabs on everything in my house and hiding from him in Publix because I didn't know the rules that governed public places put more stress on me than I knew. Maybe I didn't know how angry and scared I was. Maybe I thought I was dealing with it when I wasn't. Maybe my body rebelled against the responsibility I felt for an adult man who'd uprooted his shit life to be with a teenager and then replaced her four months later. Maybe the beat of my heart attested to what I didn't know how else to say.

DAWN LUNDY MARTIN

Mo[dern] [Frame] or a Philosophical Treatise on What Remains between History and the Living Breathing Black Human Female

After Carrie Mae Weems' Framed by Modernism (1996)

To feel a presence, they say, can be like a haunting. You are yourself and no other physical being is there, yet a feeling or sensation emerges as if from nowhere. Like The Negress. The black female body not in repose, instead walking or clickity clack. It knocks at the door, which is the surface of existence. Or, in life, it walks down the street and is asked to assume a position of slackness in response to the perception of being in perpetual heat. What would we do without her? How would we know our selves? Indeed, we need something against which the pristine can manifest itself, can create its artifice of pristineness.

To be unadorned
or unclothed—light bursts—

Glare from florescent mouths breathe their profit into me. [No one hears the glass sound of breath, just me.] Was "low," they say, "fastened in place by violence." Was "ritualized" was "debased" was "grotesque" was "black flesh" or "swathed" in "blackness, " and "finality" and "nature," was "sensualized."

In standing repose, the
object lures us into a belief that she is indeed human.
We know this from her sun-draped eyes, her capacity
for deceit. We see no absolute proof , however,
against the artist's outstretched offering—the mammy
trophy and "the fantastic Al Jolson performing his
signature tune!"

Enter machines and abstractions [zip!], automations to lengthen legs, round edges, plump buttocks. Relational fish, irrational fissure. All this shimmery ache in one place, suddenly against your back. My body aflame with it, can't you see? Make an outline around my form. Use your chisel. I will indulge your every little fit, I, your perfect muse, your fuck slut, ██████████, also your nothing.

In so far as the phrase "black woman," re-place outside of domestic "power."
I lie down in the ditch myself, stretch my body alongside the dead myself.
Outside the frame, oblique lover (De Kooning, maybe, as a young beauty),
his hand reaches in to retrieve me, and pets me, my nakedness, a fine scratch.
Filament traces in the historical body.

Representation falls away. Chokehold "blackness." Swallowed "brown." Your "black" father whose "blackness" precedes him. Stumble in laborious "black" gait toward "absence." Cross your "black" hands, empty your "black" pockets, hold your "poor" "black" baby against "brick" "wall" as instructed. And the "niggers" get "sold" up the "river" against a "lithe" "white" "fluff." You wail, a mimic-mouth into beaded rhythms of us-ness, fragrance of a cosmos where roads are not partitioned. No roads. No marks to mark up the whole big wide world, the holes of universes untethered from time. In absence of wholeness catch glimpses of the sides of selves.

If we could be without him we would. Is there any country without him? We are told of the reservoirs, that they are without sea or wind, that we attach, laconic swerve, and hold what has happened to it. Trauma sack. “What strikes me,” she says, “is how easy it is to commit atrocities.” Remove from experience, rain, un-nurture the physical form, a girl is just a girl, one ass cheek on a full chair, balancing, remove skin, water, sunlight, love, position the neck so that landscape dissolves into black wall, excise language puffs from pharynx, unfurl the scroll, hear ye hear ye.

JOYELLE MCSWEENEY

"Trial of MUSE" (from *Dead Youth, or, The Leaks*)

[Note: *Dead Youth, or, The Leaks* finds a benevolent Julian Assange piloting a stolen containership, the SS *Smirk*, on his way to Magnetic Island. His mission is to reboot a pack of DEAD YOUTH, tracksuited teens who have died by a variety of Anthropocene causes, and upload them to the Internet. The ship is boarded by two other would-be hijackers: Abduwali MUSE, a teenage Somali "pirate," and a female ST-EXUPÉRY, representing the LAW-in-travesty.

In this passage, MUSE is being tried by ST-EXUPÉRY, while the dubious YOUTH oscillate between taking the MUSE's side and that of the LAW.]

DEAD YOUTH 1: O this island. It's a pit.
DEAD YOUTH 2: It's a dump.
DEAD YOUTH 1: It's a mass grave!
DEAD YOUTH 2: Without the masses. It's deserted.
ASSANGE: Not at all. It's just the off-season. You boys play the part of the unseasonable youth. Untimely plucked. Watch out or you'll be juiced. [his tail switches like a lazy cat]

ST-EXUPÉRY: (from office area) ABDI WALI ABDULQADIR MUSE!

MUSE: I recognize the representative of France.

ST-EXUPÉRY: You are not the judge!
Nor president pro tem!
You do not recognize *me*.
Imyself am JUSTICE.
I recognize *you*.

YOUTH TO YOUTH: HUM, blind Justice recognizes Muse!
YOUTH TO YOUTH: That's what, in science, we call a *double-blind*.
TOUT YOUTH: A very pharmaceutical pursuit! Forsooth.

ST-EXUPÉRY: Silence, youth! It is golden.
It has a mouth, but it's fixed.
Like a clock, or a neutered cat,
or suit brought against an emperor.
In other words, can it.

YOUTH: Silence in other words! That is strange science!

ST-EXUPÉRY: Let the interrogation proceed. Now, Muse, I don't want to have to take out my carburetor or my salad tongs. So answer my questions. Sing, muse.

MUSE: I won't.

ST-EXUPÉRY: Then prattle.

MUSE: The only emperor is the emperor of ice cream
YOUTH: the only emperor is the emperor de glace
MUSE: the only emperor is the one who stands naked
YOUTH: the only emperor is the emperor sans pants
MUSE: and communicates to youth, directly in his nakedness.
ASSANGE: O dream of a crystalline communication.
Flap flap to dirty ears. The pidgins of pigeons.
The germs they smuggle in their penates and pinions.
The germs they share for a puddle of crumb-ions.
Good pigeons, grey matter, rats with aspirations!
O rank mass, its rank communicants! Its holy communications!
YOUTH: We Catholics believe in transubstantiation.
Our uncanny valley runs on circuits of revulsion.
MUSE: How like a thing, how like a paragon
YOUTH: how like a think, how like an epicure
MUSE: how like a stink, how like a pedicure
YOUTH: how like bacteria that thrive in the footbath
MUSE: how like a strand of flesh-eating staph
YOUTH: how like the society ladies hobble on no feet

MUSE: until they realize Jimmy Choos fit better with no feet
YOUTH: how they then occupy the lotus position
MUSE: how like a bath salt
YOUTH: how like a bidet.
MUSE: What a piece of . . . work is man
YOUTH: *Le seul empereur est l'empereur de glace*
MUSE: *Caveat emptor*
YOUTH: *Lasciate ogne speranza, voi ch'intrate.*
MUSE: Follow your leader. That's called dictee.
ST-EXUPÉRY: I see you are a very learned man.

MUSE: Maleducated. Malaparte. That's why we formed our bande à part. Before the Little Emperor could pursue his destiny, he flipped the 'Malaparte' to 'Bonaparte'. A visionary must also have a literalist's heart. And wear it like a medal on his chest.

ST-EXUPÉRY: O what a fine speech! O medals all around!

YOUTH: [affixing metals by driving pins into Muse's torso. He now resembles a Sebastian] That's tantalum, that's for capacity, in hearing aids, jet blades, and telephony. There's cassiterite that's for circuit boards. And there's wolframite that's for 'green ammunition,' i.e. bullets with less lead. So children who eat bullets won't get lead poisoning and perform poorly in standardized tests. Also good for making your iPhone vibrate.

ALL: What?

YOUTH: I kid you not. Wolframite is a very right metal. People mine each other for it. I'm talking about a combat mine, mined by gangpressed soldiers. I am not even talking about a data mine.

ASSANGE: O MUSE, you are a bouquet. You are a very directory, a very index, the very body of contemporary miseree.

ST-EXUPÉRY: That's enough. Don't encourage his vanitee. Second question. MUSE, when brought to trial in New York, why did you smile for the cameras?

MUSE: Because I have a face.
[rimshot]
[rifle crack]

ST-EXUPÉRY: WHAT'S THAT?

MUSE: Because I have a face.
ST-EXUPÉRY: OBSCENE ANSWER!

MUSE: It is the opposite of obscene. The obscene must be hidden from view. My face I show. It is a black face, but it is not in blackface. It comes from a black site. It is a leak.

ST-EXUPÉRY: O OBSCENE! O how his teeth gleams, his smile, and his eyes, his charisma, and his native talent for being alive. O obscenity. What a felony! Youth tar him with petroleum products. Then he will know what it means to be in capitalism's embrace. IN THE BOSOM OF THE LAW!

(YOUTH tar ST-EXUPÉRY instead)

WHAT? What is the meaning of this?

YOUTH: Are you not the font of Justice? I recognize you, I met you so many times on the other side of the bench. You sent me to juvie for a decade, took the kickback to buy golf clubs. Luckily I OD'd and was thus released from my sentence, albeit to the morgue. Now you wear the black robes you wore in life, which shows you have been invested with gravure as in the grave.

ST-EXUPÉRY: Well I see. Grandeur is grand. That's tautologee, a very right and total logic. Let us proceed with the proceedings. Where were we?

MUSE: You asked me why I smiled, and I replied, *because I have a face.*
ST-EXUPÉRY: Yes, yes. And yet the next day, at your trial, you wept and wept. Why did you weep?

MUSE: Because I am a teen. Because I had just learned the role cut out for me. The role of tragic youth. I didn't want it, but could not avoid it. I was trapped. And I wept because I had tears at my disposal. And I disposed of them. Or perhaps I had a grit in my eye. Perhaps I thought I could weep out an industrial diamond so tough I could use it as a weapon and cut up the court.

ST-EXUPÉRY: O, a threat! A threat against the body of the court. O what a mongrel! And yet we cannot lose our composure. As a final piece of evidence, I would like to read out something you wrote on your blog. "I think I should select from my poems as my favorite "The Emperor of Ice Cream." This wears a deliberately commonplace costume, and yet seems to me to contain something of the essential gaudiness of poetry; that is the reason why I like it."

MUSE: I wrote that?

ST-EXUPÉRY: Yes, rat, and you are trapt. You are trapt forever in your own snare because you wrote this on the Internet. It's data. It's *datestamped.*
MUSE: When did I write that?

ST-EXUPÉRY: You wrote it in 1933 in Hartford, Connecticut.
MUSE: Well, then, I denounce it. That was in my youth. Before I came into my revolutionary consciousness. Emperors indeed. Though 'the essential gaudiness of poetry' is quite a phrase, something to hold on to, to pin to the breast . . .

ST-EXUPÉRY: Your opinion about emperors has no bearing on this case. My god, you blacks. Whine whine. Somalia hasn't been ruled by an emperor for at least . . . well, *decades.* As for ice cream, typically childish. I can't understand this substance's resurgence in this play as a motif. I thought this was a play about petroleum.

DEAD YOUTH: Judge, if it please the court, I'd like to file a brief. Ice cream and petroleum are polar opposites of each other, and thus may substitute for each other, bind, and form a digital system. We pow'r this colony with the swerve, with the flip-flip. Then we can parade about in speedo's and flip-flops, and have ice-cream in the freezer and run the vacuum cleen all night. As for me, like a true hustler, I like both oil *and* ice cream. I'm ecumenical. Look, I've black nylons under my track bottoms. My jacket's so synthetic it could melt.

ST-EXUPÉRY: Silence, dead pageboys. You call that trash philosophie the 'idealism of youth'? With that kind of idealism you're more suited for a Weimar cabaretto than the Furor's youth. Now, like the Furor, let's be rational and logical. Let's review the facts of the case. Your excuse for your great crime of piracy *is your youth*. An excuse immediately invalidated by the fact that you are being tried as an adult. Therefore, ipso facto, you are no youth, therefore you are defenseless. You sir, are no youth! QED. GED. JD. STD. Associates Degree from the Lice Lycee. Also, since you refuse to ascribe to yourself a motive, I must assign one to you, and I shall select one that is more than mere larceny, which would be par de course. No, sir, let me see . . . your motive is *villainy,* villainy itself, tout court and tout de suite, and your wish to see villainy communicated to the innocent flank of the world, in the person of the MV *Maersk*, which you so wantonly call 'the *Smirk*'. O piracy! O cult of villainy! O cur! O scourge! O sturgeon with black eggs! O rub his face in shoe polish, shoe 'blacking' burnt corn cobs and ash! I should sentence you to DEATH. O, but being Just I love MERCY. So instead I shall transport you to Terre Haute, Indiana for thirty-three- and-one-third years. Don't snuffle, you'll emerge an exhausted 51. Though I dare say you'll have lost your looks.

YOUTH: No, MUSE, we will not let you perish! You or your good looks! You are a role model to us!

MUSE: DEAD YOUTH, I am not a role model. I'm not even an athlete. My only mission is not to die before my time. I wanted to say my piece, and my peace is over. And yet, I feel a tear forming right here. In these two organs which are to sight what hearing is to ears. I mean my eyes. They're pearlescing. They're dropping white bacterial wads in front of me. O I lose my vision. I am become a twin of Justice. I am a white world. I am blind.

HOLLY MELGARD[i]

Alienated Labor

George: huh uh huh
he huh uh huh

Matt: Huh uh huh he huh uh huh.
Rambo's got nothing on you, George.
Huh uh huh he huh uh huh.

George: Huh uh huh he huh.
Thank my feminine side.
Huh uh huh I was huh uh
protecting my baby
Huh uh huh he huh uh huh.

Matt: This is one way and one fifty-two.
Where the hell is my back up? Huh uh huh.
And while you're at it,
send an ambulance.

Walkie-talkie: Roger.

Matt: Huh uh ho he huh uh huh.

George: Get two—

Matt: —No, I'm ok—

George: —For me.
I'm having the baby.

Matt: No. George, you can't.

You're still in phase two.

George: It's dis-attaching

Matt: George, you told me.
You said you have two weeks left.
Whoa. WHOA!
This isn't supposed to happen.
You said you still got two weeks.

George: The fight—
It's brought on premature labor.

Matt: This is one way and one fifty two.
I also need another ambulance stat
for a delivering newcomer.
Uh, the patient is a police officer.
Get it here immediately!

Walkie-talkie: Roger.

George: We'll never make it.

Matt: Listen.
I'll get you to the birthing center.

George: Matt.
You're going to have to deliver the baby.

Matt: Come on, me?
George please please please.

George: Huh uh huh get uh huh
get me there.

Matt: George.
Why are you doing this to me?

George: Huh hah.
Huh uh hah he ha hah hah.

Matt: Why
Why
Oh why

George: Ah hah ah owe huh kuh
kuh huh oh hoh oh oh.

Matt: You know I didn't want this to happen.
You promised me, George.
Just try.

George: Hah whew hoh hah huh.

Matt: Try to hold it in.

George: I can't.
Kuh owe oh und
Undo my pants.
Huh uh huh huh oh huh.
Uh uh.

Matt: Ok alright alright
Now what?

George: Place your hands huh uh huh
here. Huh uh.

Matt: There?

George: Help me.
Help me push. Huh uh ah ahh oh oh huh uh owe oh!

Matt: George?

George: Ah ahhhhh.
Push.

Matt: George—

George: —Push! Oh ugh.

Matt: Ok, ok.
Just hang in there.
All right?

George: And now,
push your fists against my temples.
It helps dilate the pouch.
Huh huh huh uh huh.

Matt: How's that?
Huh?

George: Uh huh haaaah. Oh hoh uh huh.
Huh.
Huh uh huh he huh.
It's coming. Huh huh
It's
It's coming.

Matt: What do I do
what do I do?
George?

George: Huh oh huh oh huh uh huh huh
oh push.
Push.

Matt: Grrr
Wuh—

George: Huh uh.
Breath.

Matt: Hoo hoo shoo who hoo hoo.
Ok
I'm ok.
I'm ok.

George: Push!
Oh aaaaaaaaaaah!

Matt: George?
What.

George: Napul rotay [click]

Matt: What's that?

George: Breath but. Cuh

Matt: —Oh man—

George: —guhhh she . . .
She can't get out.

Matt: What could I do?
What can I do?
What do I do, George George talk to me.

George!
Don't you check out on me.

George: Matt . . . the baby . . . I can feel it dying . . . Guhh huhhh . . .

Matt: George—George!
Wake up. George!
Oh my god.
The baby—it's still not. George wake up.

George: . . .

Matt: COME ON

George: Guh huh

Matt: It's all right.
It's gonna be ok.
I've got it. Cha hah.
Here we go. Here we go.
It's coming out. Come on come on.
Ok. Here we go. It's your girl, she's coming out.

George: Ahhhhh!

Matt: George—Oh god.
George: Huh uh huh uh uh . . . turn . . . her . . . face… up . . . turn . . . her . . .

Fesna: Oh ah ah ahhhh wow ha ah awah

Matt: Oh George! She's beautiful. She's beautiful! Ha ha

George: ha ha huh ha ha huh ha

Fesna: Ilah owe ah ah huh ha ahhhh

George: Fesna! Fesna!
She huh hah huh
She has Susan's spots.
Oh Fesna.

Matt: Huh ha ha hah. She's cold.

George: She needs the comfort of two bodies
Huh ah ha uh huh uh huh. Huh
Her mother isn't here.
Huh uh huh
Matt, lie close to us—

Matt: —Huh uh huh huh huh uh huh

George: Fesna ha ha huh I want you to meet
your godfather

George, Matt, & Fesna:
Hah huh uh huh ah ha ha ah wuh huh haaa.

---

[i] Transcription Source:

tovasshi. "Alien Nation – Birth Scene." *Youtube*. Youtube, 13 April, 2008. Web. January 5, 2013.[1]

[1] Youtube Clip Source:

"Real Men." *Alien Nation*. Episode 17, Season 1. 20th Century Fox. 19 February, 1990.

TYLER MILLS

H-Bomb

We could not calculate directions between Johnson, VT, and Elugelab.

We could not calculate directions between Tokyo, Japan, and Elugelab.

Search nearby, e.g., "pizza."

Your search for "pizza" near Elugelab, Enewetak Atoll, RMI, did not match any locations.

Make sure all words are spelled correctly.

Did you mean Marshall Islands resort?

We could not calculate directions between Marshall Islands and Elugelab.

The blast will come out of the horizon just about *there*.

Welcome aboard the USS Estes.

You have a grandstand seat here to see one of the most momentous events in the history of science.

It is now thirty seconds to zero time.

Know about this place and want everyone to find it?

If the reactor goes, we are in the thermonuclear era.

You are about to add a place that you believe is missing so everyone can find it.

Put on goggles or turn away.

Do not face the burst until ten seconds after the first light.

Enter a place name: [a few dozen neutrons].

We do not support adding a place here.

Refresh.

Enter a place name: [water furred with wind].

Refresh.

ELENA MINOR

rrs FEED

the passing of a poet is
never a small cry / es

llanto para ahogar
un mar

sendero voraz—

titanic roar—
—din of refraction at the
red-eyed rim of the universe y más—allá . . .

. . . a great maw that words a-loud
a-lone
can b/reach.

↓

so *¡shout holler & h* o w *l!* youz
s[p]inners :—: st[r]ump &
[s]crawl it
crack the beveled element
wind the ballin' clock
keen the whip of coda

cross & cross & cross again / (repeat)

canta pueblo . . . canta

hasta la última gota primera palabra y

punto

sin fin ∞ al[l]
for poets [who] die [*sin song*] every day

NICK MONTFORT

Through the Park

```
#!/usr/bin/python
import random, textwrap
for i in range(0, 8):
    text = ["The girl grins and grabs a granola bar",
    "The girl puts on a slutty dress",
    "The girl sets off through the park",
    "A wolf whistle sounds",
    "The girl turns to smile and wink",
    "The muscular man paces the girl",
    "Chatter and compliments cajole",
    "The man makes a fist behind his back",
    "A wildflower nods, tightly gripped",
    "A snatch of song reminds the girl of her grandmother",
    "The man and girl exchange a knowing glance",
    "The two circle",
    "Laughter booms",
    "A giggle weaves through the air",
    "The man's breathing quickens",
    "A lamp above fails to come on",
    "The man dashes, leaving pretense behind",
    "Pigeons scatter",
    "The girl runs",
    "The man's there first",
    "Things are forgotten in carelessness",
    "The girl's bag lies open",
    "Pairs of people relax after journeys and work",
    "The park's green is gray",
    "A patrol car's siren chirps"]
    phrases = 7 + random.randint(0,4)
```

```
while len(text) > phrases:
    text.remove(random.choice(text))
print "\n[" + str(i+1) + "]\n\n" + \
    textwrap.fill(". ... ".join(text) + ".", 60) + "\n\n\n"
```

[1]

The girl grins and grabs a granola bar. . . . The girl puts on a slutty dress. . . . The girl turns to smile and wink. . . . The man makes a fist behind his back. . . . A snatch of song reminds the girl of her grandmother. . . . Laughter booms. . . . The man's breathing quickens. . . . Pigeons scatter. . . . The girl runs. . . . Things are forgotten in carelessness. . . . The girl's bag lies open.

[2]

The girl grins and grabs a granola bar. . . . The girl turns to smile and wink. . . . A giggle weaves through the air. . . . The man's breathing quickens. . . . Pigeons scatter. . . . The man's there first. . . . Things are forgotten in carelessness. . . . The park's green is gray. . . . A patrol car's siren chirps.

[3]

A wolf whistle sounds. . . . The muscular man paces the girl. . . . The man makes a fist behind his back. . . . A wildflower nods, tightly gripped. . . . The two circle. . . . The man's there first. . . . Things are forgotten in carelessness. . . . The girl's bag lies open. . . . The park's green is gray.

[4]

A wildflower nods, tightly gripped. . . . The two circle. . . . The man's breathing quickens. . . . A lamp above fails to come on. . . . The man dashes, leaving pretense behind. . . . Pigeons scatter. . . . The girl runs. . . . The girl's bag lies open. . . . The park's green is gray.

[5]

The girl grins and grabs a granola bar. . . . The girl puts on a slutty dress. . . . A wolf whistle sounds. . . . The girl turns to smile and wink. . . . Chatter and compliments cajole. . . . The man makes a fist behind his back. . . . A snatch of song reminds the girl of her grandmother. . . . The man and girl exchange a knowing glance. . . . Laughter booms. . . . The man's breathing quickens.

[6]

The girl sets off through the park. . . . A wolf whistle sounds. . . . The girl turns to smile and wink. . . . The muscular man paces the girl. . . . A wildflower nods, tightly gripped. . . . The man and girl exchange a knowing glance. . . . Laughter booms. . . . A giggle weaves through the air. . . . The man dashes, leaving pretense behind. . . . Pigeons scatter. . . . Things are forgotten in carelessness.

[7]

The girl puts on a slutty dress. . . . A wolf whistle sounds. . . . The muscular man paces the girl. . . . Chatter and compliments cajole. . . . A snatch of song reminds the girl of her grandmother. . . . Laughter booms. . . . The man dashes, leaving pretense behind. . . . The man's there first. . . . Things are forgotten in carelessness. . . . Pairs of people relax after journeys and work.

[8]

The girl puts on a slutty dress. . . . The man makes a fist behind his back. . . . A snatch of song reminds the girl of her grandmother. . . . The man and girl exchange a knowing glance. . . . A giggle weaves through the air. . . . The man's breathing quickens. . . . The girl runs. . . . Things are forgotten in carelessness.

FRED MOTEN

harriot + harriott + sound +

The pitch and time of luters
bring atlantic situations
all the way across. the moon
thing is a water thing at
midnight and the table
burst with variation.
the beautiful riot say
I'm not like this and
walk away embrace and
dig up under normandie.
what's a black singing body
got to do with it? look at
my shoes. the setting partly frees
the dissonance in compensation
and tsitsi ella jaji frees the rest.
frayed means are a thingly
jingly nette; you can't help
yourself if you take too much.

DANIEL NADLER

from "The Lacunae"

NOTE. THESE TEXTS ARE IMAGINED translations of poems that do not otherwise exist. They are intended to fill invented or actual lacunae in manuscripts of first- to eighth-century CE classical Indian poetry (*Amarusataka*, originally in Sanskrit; *Kuruntokai*, originally in Old Tamil; and *Gathasaptasati*, originally in Maharastri Prakrit).

43.71

What will you do with these pearls he has given you?
Can you eat them? Can you grind them into honey
and return them to the water, sweeter than they were?
Your neck is not a graveyard for the sea.
So don't become a ghost
that scares away
the fish you must catch for your parents.

(*Amarusataka* 8.9, Sanskrit)

51.30

Who are you going to meet tonight
in the tall grass
where even snakes cannot find each other?

Your bare feet
will be the safest part of you.

(*Gathasaptasati* 10.95, Prakrit)

28.6

I want to boast
around you, like a horse rearing straight up
in the stars.

But I have nothing to say.
Like the night
when the moon is out.

(*Amarusataka* 1.12, Sanskrit)

22.0

My tigers have left me.
I wake too late in the day,
after a heavy rain
has played its notes on my roof.
I don't even tie them to anything.

(*Gathasaptasati* 18.46, Prakrit)

17.15

Between kisses the air is quiet,
like trees after a snowfall. Talking softly, after,
a branch is shaken loose.

(*Gathasaptasati* 7.38, Prakrit)

15.24

The moon has gone farming at night
in the soil of your dreams. Tall trees
are growing there, for you to climb,
and the flower I gave you during the day
can barely break through the ground.

(*Amarusataka* 30, Sanskrit)

15.34

You disappear beside me in a forest. Walking, I cannot hear
the moment when fewer leaves are crushed, and I speak to you
as if it made no difference that the forest listened in your place.

For you I learned
that what is near us is never what is near us.

(*Amarusataka* 30, Sanskrit)

18.0

Do not let the thought of her fill your nights
and the stars
pieces of her.

Come,
we will walk through the streets, and find a table
that doesn't even look like her.

(*Amarusataka* 32.2, Sanskrit)

15.29

Like wooden planks from a broken ship
dashed against great stones,
my words you made into a spectacle
for the whole village to attend. I only meant to tell you
I love another.

(*Amarusataka* 30, Sanskrit)

15.32

Your lips are as full as the wound
guarded in battle. Your skin is the color of my eyelids when the sun passes through.
The sea takes my shape as I float in it,
your hair falls all around you, like the paths of gravity made visible.

(*Amarusataka* 30, Sanskrit)

38.90

You hear the sun in the morning
through closed shutters. As you sleep
the early sky is colored
in fish scales, and you open your eyes
like a street
already lined with fruit.

(*Amarusataka* 3.89, Sanskrit)

SUNNY NAGRA

The Old Man and the Peach Tree

Having gone left when it is dictated that a right must be made at The Peach Tree In Bloom, The Old Man becomes lost in The Forest of Everything. The *waama*[1] path is not marked for him; The Old Man is right-handed. Both The Trees and The Wind know of this, of both his lostness and his right-handedness; but The Old Man refuses to ask for help, partially because:

1) Willingness to ask for directions is negatively correlated with penis-size[2] and The Old Man is—**ahem**—well, we all have our shortcomings.

And partially because:

2) The Properties of the Place ordain that The Old Man receive no help[3] even though The Trees are eager to give it should it be asked for and The Wind, while reluctant, is also willing.

Instead, he must walk aimlessly, praying for cloud coverage. Without The Moon & The Stars, The Old Man finds himself walking in circles[4], hoping that the center holds so that he can make his way back to The Peach Tree, which is also The Door Back[5] but only when visited for the Second Time[6].

Maybe it has to do with The Place or The Circles but some nights it almost seems endless. That for The Old Man, it does not seem that he's walked one circle or two or even dozens. The circles feel infinite and The Old Man fears he will die like this, walking around in these circles. It is also unclear what effect counterclockwise circles have on The Forest of Everything but backward expressions of Time are Unnatural, regardless of place. The Operations of Time here are, for the most part, unknown. Even on nights when The Old Man walks so much that blisters form and break on his feet and his lips are chapped to cracks (It feels like days have progressed sometimes), the night is still soaked with darkness[7] when he gets back to his bed and falls asleep. Whenever The Peach Tree comes back to sight The Old Man's heart always twists and the fear of dying here is replaced with the fear of returning back to bed[8].

And now he fears that he shouldn't have gone left, that he has doomed himself by doing so and he is almost certain that he will never see The Peach Tree again and that is when Naga[9] appears[10]. Naga looms fearsome in snake-form and asks, "Who are you?" The Old Man trembles and Naga asks, "Why are you here?"

"I'm lost," The Old Man says.

"Oh," replies Naga. "Well, who isn't experiencing some existential dread, the times being what they are and all?"

"No," The Old Man says, "I don't know how to get back."

"Why would you want to go back?"

"I'm scared of dying here."

"What of dying elsewhere?"

"That scares me, too."

"Then why not die here?"

"When I'm here, I'm more aware."

"That's the Nature of the Place."

The Old Man looks at Naga and he knows this place is not a dream[11] as he sometimes wishes it to be. He always knew but his type of knowing has transformed. Before it was an Inside Knowing, a knowing that he could never give voice to, even within his mind but now it has become an Outside Knowing, a knowing that has words his mind's eye can see and that his mouth can form. He says it out loud: "This is not a Dream."

"No," Naga says, "It is not." The Old Man begins to wonder if here he is already dead and that's what he's been doing every night that he can't sleep: Dying and Coming Back again and again. This is bad because he'll never die this way, not in a real sense[12] that is. He thinks of his grandma and how after his grandfather's death she said she was going to live forever. That her True Time was before him and now it would never happen and The Old Man remembers how throughout his childhood she became more wizened and thin, stick-like, with age carving lines in her face like rough bark, her hair beginning to stick up like leaves. He remembers thinking that she resembled a tree.

"Grandma?" The Old Man whispers looking around at The Forest.

"I'm not your Grandma," Naga says.

"No," The Old Man says, "You're not."

"Why would you call me that? I am Naga, mighty and strong. Not an old lady."

"No. I was just thinking of my grandmother."

"I remind you of your Grandmother? A wispy, old tree-like figure? Look at the size of me!"

"No, that's not what I meant."

"That's what you said. I'm fearsome. I could eat you."

"No!"

"No? You command me? You believe you have authority over me?"

"No—I meant no as in don't." But the words are lost in Naga's rage and The Old Man knows this so he turns to run while The Great Serpent God uncoils himself to give pursuit, his jaws opening wide enough to swallow The Moon & The Sea, The Earth & The Sun, The Universe & All Its Infinities.

Footnotes

1. "In *Sanskriti*, the word waama stands for both 'left' and 'wicked.'" (http://en.wikipedia.org/wiki/Bias_against_left-handed_people)

2. Road rage and the need to construct and adhere to a stringent concept of masculinity are also negatively correlated. Some scientists also suspect a correlation with Anger and Humor but research still needs to be done. Various sources say the quadratic formula[1] and matrices are being employed[2].

3. At least not from The Trees or The Wind.

4. "The results, published today in the journal, *Current Biology*, showed that no matter how hard people tried to walk in a straight line, they often ended up going in circles without ever realizing that they were crossing their own paths. But there was a twist. Circular walking befell only the four forest walkers who had to walk in overcast conditions and the one desert walker who walked at night after the moon had set. Those who could see the sun or moon managed to travel fairly straight."[3] http://news.discovery.com/human/evolution/walking-circles.htm

5. Who comes up with these things? Other answers I[4] want include:

What constitutes a happy life?

Why The Old Man gets up around two every night to walk these circles in The Forest of Everything, tissues in pocket because cold, moonlit air makes his nose dribble that liquidy stuff that's not mucus but he's not really sure what the medical term is. I know part of it's because he's terrified, that laying in bed strikes through him an agony like being paralyzed and submerged in water but what is the name of the sensation, the name of the agony[5]?

How does one go about determining and fulfilling the soul's ambition?

How to tell if someone's really listening, like Deep Down Listening?

Is asking someone to marry you and expecting them to fulfill that commitment to their dying breaths an inherently selfish act?

Is all love selfish?[6]

Are there ways of loving that aren't?

How?

6. When visited for the second time, The Peach Tree ceases to be in bloom.

7. He cannot check the bedside alarm because he got rid of it when his sleep troubles first started. People saying that the light is bad and whatnot. He's too exhausted to look for clocks elsewhere.

8. It's to be noted that he has no trouble falling asleep once he gets to his bed, it's just more the sense that he *fears* he will have trouble. So it goes.

9. "Naga is theSanskritand Pāliword for a deity or class of entity or being, taking the form of a very great snake—specifically the king cobra, found in Hinduism, Buddhism, Jainism andSikhism. A female Nāga is anāgīor nāginī." (http://en.wikipedia.org/wiki/naga)

10. The Old Man has never seen Naga before and suspects it has something to do with the *waama* path.

11. And how could it ever be a dream? Doesn't every piece of writing have some contract with the reader? Doesn't that contract become null and void when the writing resorts to the cliché to end? (The surrealist qualities of this work make a dream a possibility but one could object to that stating that all works of surrealism should not necessarily be read as dreams even though they seek to replicate some of the harsher elements of dreaming such as an underlying paranoia that something is seeking to do them harm.)[7]

12. Whatever that means.

2nd Set of Footnotes (Contains Footnotes for the First Set of Footnotes)

1. x equals negative b plus or minus the square root of b square minus 4ab all over 2a.

2. These are—as far as it is known—made-up statistics.

3. It's doubtful that The Old Man knows the science behind it but he does have the belief that it has something to do with sight. The Old Man thinks that maybe closing his eyes would help get him back but he is too terrified to do so[1].

4. I refers to |The Speaker As Prophet Blessed With The Sight of The *Tiseree Ankh*[2]|[3].

5. Would naming it help?[4]

6. Google "Reminder" by Michael Ryan.

7. For examples of weak endings see: most movies with twists near the climax and how very often they seem a cop out and show The Screenwriter's lack of skill and/or unwillingness to sit down with the art piece and grind it out[5] (which can also be called a skill)[6].

3rd Set of Footnotes (Contains Footnotes for the Second Set of Footnotes)

1. It is also unclear if it is the humanistic tendency to walk in circles that guides him back or if something else is at work due to The Properties of the Place.

2. Third Eye.

3. Though not true in all cases, The Speaker's Sight is limited. There exist Gaps in Knowledge.

4. Both The Old Man and I don't think so. The only cure that The Old Man envisions working would be telling someone about this (but The Old Man is scared that they wouldn't really listen, like Deep Down Listen (where The Listener strives for Pain Acknowledgement[1] on an Empathetic-Level; where they have to imagine the other person as Real as they see themselves in order to conjure up The Hurt) and The Old Man knows that the only way that the cure would work would be if the other person was Deep Down Listening.)

5. This happens when the writer puts aside their own notions of what they want the art piece to be. Instead of seeing the art as Of Themself, they should try to imagine it as something apart

in order to determine what the art piece needs and then try to help it achieve this. This is not an Act of Detachment or Push for Objectivity but an Attempt at Empathy with the piece, which is an extension of emotion. Parents do something similar. This is a subcategory of Deep-Down Listening. A Good Parent is a Good Deep-Down Listener.

6. In The Screenwriter's Defense he was scared of touching the piece, scared that touching it would ruin what was good about the it[2].

4th Set of Footnotes (You Know the Drill)

1. Because that's the worst part of it: If The Old Man could get The Listener to understand one thing it would be how it hurts, that the way that the fear grips him is almost physical, so strong is his terror.

2. This is only an allowable defense if The Screenwriter still claims Amateurship. It is unclear if The Screenwriter is still an amateur, because they're getting paid so in one sense they are not an amateur but whether or not they've fulfilled The Apprenticeship of Their Craft is unclear[1].

5th Set of Footnotes

1. How one does so (fulfill apprenticeship) is not decreed in the way that Right Turns in The Forest of Everything are because Criteria and Rules are generally only good for Snobs. For the Unsnobivifed it is sufficient to say that You[1]'ll Know It When You See It[2]. Or rather when you *feel* it; you'll listen to its vibrations but in any case, General Symptoms of Apprenticeship include:

   1. Crises of Self and how Self relates to Art and Art to Self.[3]
   2. Being in Solular Flux[4].
   3. It is also said that it gets lonely (You hope that this is not true or at the very least that it is the type of loneliness that is bearable).

   General Symptoms of Apprenticeship will not go away but there is a transition between Aspiring and Actualized and much grey area in-between and around the whole thing.

6th Set of Footnotes

1. You refers to |Young Human as Aspiring Artist|.

2. Which also happens to be the Supreme Court's take on porn[1].

3. Like when you're thinking about the relationship between being a Good Person and a Good Artist:

because you've just heard about Fitzgerald and how he treated Zelda[2], how he practically fucked with her mind just to see her reaction and write it down and you decide that's not something you're ever going to do for Art. You're never going to do that to someone you say you love because you're trying to be a better older brother and you're not enough for him right now, like the way you want to be because right now you're not enough even for yourself. You know this because summer came and you were back home and angry[3] and you knew why you were angry and that you shouldn't be but that didn't help[4]. It also didn't help that the anger felt good in a way. And then you blinked and summer diappeared[5]. You're asking yourself if you really want this because if you did then you wouldn't have blinked; you'd've stared summer down and not be here asking yourself what you're doing[6].

You think about the relationship between Good Person and Good Artist, again:

When you read That Poet. The one that everyone loves and That Poet is Good, like objectively

Good and you can see their skill but you try to avoid their poetry[7] and not get any of their books because whenever you read their poetry you Identify Too Much with some of those feelings and they're feelings you don't want to Identify With. So you're avoiding writing Those Poems because Writing has a way of making certain things permanent in a way that Thinking doesn't and you wonder if that's what happened to That Poet: too many people were telling them how Good it was and so why change if you can make Art? You think they got stuck because they're still writing Those Poems (They're Different (of course) and Show Growth of Poetic Skill but The Ache[8] is Still The Same).

You find Hope in Czeslaw Milosz's Poetry. It's Pulsation you read as Personal Salvation. When Grown you want to see Former Self (you at the present) with the Healing Balm his words make you believe he's found. Milosz's Backward Gaze at his Old Self reveals you, Mirrored & Aching.

You taste The Change in The Gaze[9] and it leaves you envy-filled, telling Self to be patient. It's that Change that That Poet couldn't seem to find nor likely will[10].

4. So· u· lar Flux: *made-up term*

Definition:

1. A certain state of the soul, in which the soul is open to being moldable; open to change.

2. State in which parts of the soul (like the artistic part) are still being formed and shaped.

Used in a sentence: Under Apprenticeship of the Craft, one should be in Soular Flux in order to be influenced by different methods and movements of Writing. Mixing them together and adding Self forms the Artist's Style.

7th Set of Footnotes

1. Two things about this fact:

   1. This fact is, in fact, a fact.

   2. Does this mean that the Supreme Court isn't a snob about porn? This is probably for the best: Porn Snobs rank ahead of even Film Snobs and Rap Snobs on The Big-Ass List of Worst Snobs to Interact With.

2. And who the fuck cares? What is this TMZ?—but you do. You don't know why.
3. Like burn the world down angry[1].
4. Anger closes all three eyes. You know this and that doesn't help either.
5. Anger has a weird way of erasing time.
6. What are you doing, anyway?[2]
7. They seem to pop up a lot though. That's the way it goes with things you want to avoid.
8. When you read the poems you're scared that The Ache won't ever go away.
9. And he does this without denying True Self:

   Which is what you fear you're doing by not writing Those Poems.

   Which is the one thing about That Poet's Writing that you covet:

   Not their world-class skill but their Honesty.

10. Look: The Thing is: you can't Prove It. Any of it. You can't graph this out or show someone where the Healing Balm is or quantify it or prove it in "An Essay" using "Literary Criticism". Honestly a better argument could be made in Opposition. Someone could pull out That Poet's Poetry and point to places and be like: "See, they're trying to Change here" and that person would be right but you Feel when you Read It that the Change is only at a surface level, like not truly engaged in the way someone needs to be; in the way you need to be. You don't know exactly how to explain it—

It's like when Murakami writes about how listening to Bob Dylan is like watching rain fall and you can't show someone the raindrops in Dylan's music[3]. And so you start thinking that if you can't *Prove It* Prove It, then in a way how are you suppose to Feel It? If your only proof is Read This and if that person doesn't feel the same way then you have to tell them that you can't explain it in words and if you can't do that then is it Real? And you think: *Yeah, it is.* You think (and excuse your language): *Fuck An Essay: it's Real, it's as real as anything is going to be for you.*[4]

8th Set of Footnotes

1. Metaphorically that is. You're not like a pyromaniac or a psychopath or anything. You don't want to hurt anyone.

2. Dying from mortality[1].

3. Metaphorically that is. You're sure the word "raindrops" appears *a lot.*

4. But the thing is: Even this makes you feel bad because one of the Worst Feelings you know is when you're talking to your little brother and he Shuts You Out. Like there will be a point in the conversation and past that point you know he's not listening and no matter what words come out of your mouth he won't even try to understand what you're trying to say to him[2]. You feel Isolated because you have all these words but they're Useless. Not being able to communicate the thoughts you have inside you to another is in your mind a step closer to Solipsism (which is a place you don't want to go[3]). You fear the feeling your brother gives you is the same one you give to another when you say you can't Explain why Writing makes you Feel what it does.

9th Set of Footnotes

1. No, like on Tuesday. Do you have any plans for your Birthday? The big two one. You gotta get shit-faced.

2. There's this picture you saw on Instagram that shows someone adamantly talking to a brick wall (with hand gestures and everything) and the picture is captioned: "When you're trying to convince your mother that she's wrong".

3. Even That Poet's wary of Solipsism. It's just Bad News all around.

KELLY NELSON

*TH*INK*ING, TANG*LING *SHADOWS*

Think

of

Your

life

a s

The

long

blue

dance

un

burying

Who you are

mi cielo

*vid*a m*is*

*L*a lámp*ara*

*so*lit*arios*

la red *de*

*m*i cam*ino*

a *es*toy

profundas *lo*s camp*os*
*l*a *bo*ca d*el* viento.

*nad*i*e*

existías.

A*quí*

*pá*jar*os*

*arremol*in*a*

Tú estás aquí.
*Tú me res*pond*erás*

*Aqu*í *te* am*o*

errant*es*

*A veces u*na ve*la*

Aquí te am*o*

barcos grave*s,*

*quieren cant*ar t*u nombre*

MENDI + KEITH OBADIKE

The Wash House

Each load holds
its unique weight,
its own singular stink,
some curious stain,
left to spoil some
body's favorite pants.

There is an art to
driving filth from any
matter in the sink.
Hardest is the one
for chasing blood
from human hands.

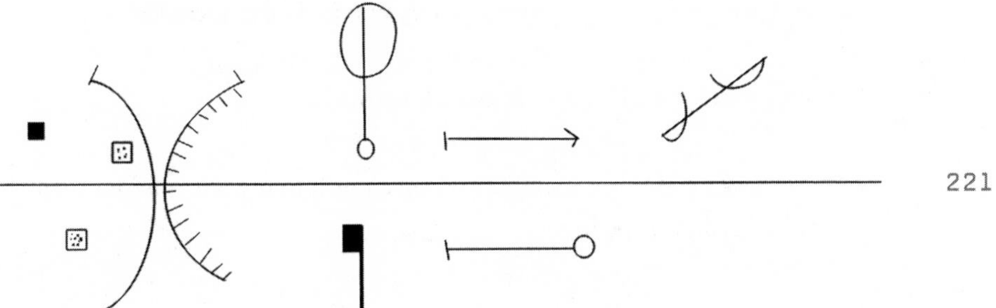

THE WASH HOUSE

needs[1]*: a white shirt; an iron; a metal tub; water; soap; coins; a stained white sheet; clothing, including at least one red article for which the color runs; laundry soap; a white rug; a room with white cabinets; a dark, greasy substance; coins; indigo or indigo-colored dye; a slavery era disclosure document*

1. Using an iron, burn a cross into a white shirt.

2. Make sudsy water in a metal tub. Drop coins into it. Stare into the soap until you can see the money.

3. Try to wash the stain from a stained white sheet.

4. Wet the clothing. Wring it out and make a tower of laundry.

5. On a dark surface, write the word "trouble" using laundry soap.

6. Wash a red article of clothing until the color runs. Hang the dripping clothing to dry over a white rug.

7. Open the cabinets. Dirty your hands with a dark, greasy substance. Make a mark on the inside of each of the cabinet doors.

8. Drop laundry soap onto a dark surface. Hide coins in it.

9. Soak your hands in indigo-colored water for one hour. Take them out. Repeat until they are blue and wrinkled.

10. Acquire a slavery era disclosure document from a corporation that has profited from slavery. Dip it into sudsy water and wash away the history.

LANCE OLSEN

dreamlives of debris: an excerpt

> *Someone, I tell you, in another time will remember us,*
> *but never as who we were.*
> *—Sappho*

:::: debris

I have my doll and the screamings behind my eyelids. The screamings look like fluttery lights. The fluttery lights believe they live inside me, but I live inside them, too.

My doll's name is Catastrophe.

:::: debris

Daddy once made his ideas purer than King Aegeus's. Now every year King Aegeus sends seven of his bravest young men and seven of his most beautiful young women from Athens to Crete to visit me. I let them wander the passages of my heart for hours—or maybe it is days, or weeks—I do not know what any of these words mean—before I step out of their frothy panic to welcome them.

:::: debris

I say *once*, I say *now*, I say *hours, days, weeks*, but I do not understand myself: down here time is a storm-swarmed ship always breaking up.

:::: debris

The liquid architecture will not hold still. Sometimes I cannot locate the walls. I shuffle forward, hands outstretched in the grainy charcoal air, breathing mold, must, fungus, sulfur, damp dirt, wet rock, waiting for the gritty touch ushering me onto the far shore. Sometimes so many walls erupt around me I am forced to crab sideways to make any progress at all.

Sometimes the walls become a whirlwind of hands or dying alphabets.

The ceiling sinks without warning and I discover myself crawling on my belly across the chalky floor, Catastrophe clutched tight to my chest.

:::: debris

Remember, angel, mommy whispers, rocking me in her lap, *you do not need to learn to adapt to Daedalus's imagination. Survival is never mandatory.*

:::: debris

Despite my height, I should mention, my strength is not negligible.

Last month—no, last year—next—I am not sure—I am never sure—no surprises there—one always knows a sliver less than one did a flinch ago—at some point in timelessness mommy and daddy gave me a little sister to play with.

Our wrestling match persisted the length of one short startled bleat.

Since then I have been an only child again.

:::: debris

Apis the Healer tells me I am thirty-three years old. I cannot remember. He tells me nobody believed I would live past thirty-three months.

This, he says, is why mommy calls me Her Little Duration.

Why daddy calls me The Minotaur.

I call myself Debris.

:::: debris

When I set out to greet my new guests I tuck my doll beneath my arm and carry a torch. This is not so I can see them. It is so they can see me.

The brave young men, unarmed, unnerved, usually shit or piss themselves a little when I step into the open. I think they are expecting someone else. It is not un-amusing to watch their secretions trickling down their legs as they blunder into blank walls trying to un-see me.

All I have to do is stand there clearing my throat.

Matters usually take care of themselves.

I follow the women like their own shadows, torchless. They cannot hear me, have no sense of my presence, until they feel me clambering up their backs, hands searching for necks, teeth for arteries.

:::: debris

What I am telling you, I want to say, is a love story.

:::: debris

Search as I might over the years, if one may call them that, and not something else—miscalculations, for instance—I have never ferreted out the guarded portal. Surely it exists in the same way, say, future dictionaries exist.

:::: debris

Our virtuoso artificer Daedalus designed my palace.

Mommy says upon its completion he could barely find his own way out.

His brilliance lives inside the body of a pasty man-sized toad sans ass who wears the perpetual grimace of a Skeptic. I have never seen him smile. His rumpled face carries the same message wherever it goes:

Stand a little less between me and the darkness.

:::: debris

I often wake alarmed from the noise they call sleep. My world becomes all blackness and rabbit snifts. I wonder if everyone has forgotten me.

How long has it been since mommy rocked Her Little Duration? Since the eunuch priests loosed a pig covered with sacrificial ribbons to snort its scramble through my heart?

How long has it been since my trough was refreshed? My favorite

amphora—teeming with the taste of violets, hyacinths, and interesting injuries—hidden like a gift for me to root out?

When all instants fuss behind your eyelids at once they become shiny fracas.

Then they become me.

:::: debris

And then mommy brought around Lady Tiresias.

Calling my name, listening for my response, she zeroed in on her princess.

Soon the three of us were sitting cross-legged in a chamber I had never seen before. It stank of language.

Vowels, mostly.

The blind bony seer with wrinkled female dugs has known life as both man and woman. He had my pity. She reached for my hand. He wanted to read my palm. I hissed at her. He drew back.

Mommy stroked my scruff.

Be nice, button, she said.

Lady Tiresias tried again. She discovered my palm bloated smooth as a baboon's ass: no bumps, lumps, fissures, figures, failures, futures.

You are born, she said, of a very special race. The Minotaur belongs to a people old as the earth itself. Beneath the skin of your shoulders grow wings. Someday they will break out and carry you far away from here.

I reached back, felt nothing.

Give yourself time, she said. The number thirty-three controls your life. You are concerned not with personal ambition but with uplifting the loving energy of humankind.

Out the corner of my eye I saw mommy shift awkwardly.

Lady Tiresias's bald head reminded me of an enormous gland.

You are a born leader, he said. This is what I see. You will achieve great fame through kindness, tenderness, compassion. Remember: whosoever is delighted in solitude is a god. Lady Tiresias has spoken.

:::: debris

These speech turbulences are not mine—do not seem to be mine, do and do not seem to be mine. That is, I am nearly convinced my mouth is vigorously un-moving as I ramble these branchings.

(I have just tapped it with my hoof for proof.)

:::: debris

That is, I sometimes have the impression I exist.

:::: athena chorus

:::: debris

I should mention minotaurs have nothing to do with the perpetuation of life. The very idea of multiplication disgusts us.

:::: debris

If I am not the only numerous.

:::: debris

That afternoon mommy led the unsuspecting blind man to the Brazen Bull. The hollow bronze beast hulked on a raised platform in our central courtyard at the edge of the shallow pool swarming with eels, each fitted with a pair of tiny gold earrings. Two Athenian slaves helped him through the hatch in its side. Lady Tiresias ordered them to be careful. They obeyed. Crouching here in the darkness I watched them light the fire. It quickly crackled into consciousness. Soon clouds of incense were shooting from the bull's nostrils. The complex system of tubes and stops inside its skull translated the soothsayer's shrieks into infuriated bovine bellows.

:::: debris

First comes pain, whispers mommy, rocking, *then knowledge*.

:::: debris

Next day they opened the hatch and extracted what was left of Lady Tiresias. Mommy asked the most delicate bits be fashioned into my beautiful new bracelet.

Mommy loves Her Little Duration.

:::: debris

Before that and after that I watched many wars. Or maybe it was the same war many times. Before that and after that I watched the elaborate festival at which daddy wedded his queen, whose own daddy tainted her with the same witchery with which she tainted me. Before that and after that I watched the slow wreckage of my city bog into the earth. Before that and after that I watched Daedalus's boy attempt to scrabble up a hidden ladder above a seascape like hammered silver, his wax wings reducing to air around him. Before that and after that I watched my sister Ariadne, whom I have never met, hand something I could not make out to a muscular young man I could not recognize standing in front of a gate I could not place. Before that and after that I watched daddy, whom I have never met, reclining in a silver bathtub decorated with octopi and anemones. I watched the daughter of Cocalus, King of Camicus, signal her slave to empty a pot not of warm water but of boiling oil over his head and chest and groin. Before that and after that I watched me hanging weightless in mommy's womb, strangling my almost-brother with his own umbilical cord, preparing to bestow upon my parents' my first gift, which they would in turn mummify and boon back to me, a mutual sign of our abiding affection.

(This was back when hope still helped.)

:::: debris

There are the stories that make sense. These are called lies. There are the stories that maze you. These are called the world.

I should mention your body is a haunted house you can't escape.

:::: debris

Which is to say the worst is still to come, was still to come, will still be to come, has come, had come, is coming, has been coming, might come, is going to come, will have come, would have come, but not yet, and already.

:::: j. g. ballard song

Because all clocks are labyrinths.

:::: lady tiresias chorus

When I die, it will have been inside the stomach of a bull. When I die, it will have been inside the courtyard of a doomed palace. When I die, it will have been with the understanding that the descent into Hades is the same from every point, every race, every gender, every class, every ancestry. With the recognition I will soon meet Odysseus in the infinite gray desert of the afterness and, skin ashen, eyes cloudy and blank from too much seeing, violet mouth sewn shut with black catgut, he will ask me sans voice to recollect for him what the best path of life is. Standing alone with the sacker of cities, I will advise him to forget the philosophers, ignore their metaphysics, for in the end there exists nothing save atoms and empty space—that is it, that is all, that is us, that is this. No one will arrive to save us from ourselves. When I die, it will have been wondering whether I am actually thinking these thoughts I think I am thinking or only dreaming I am thinking them as I study the glowing blue flame float out from my chest and across a black ocean, how it must at some point have ceased to be part of me and become part of something else, for it is so far away, and then farther, and th

:::: jorge luis borges song

Because time is a river which sweeps me along, but I am the river; it is a tiger which destroys me, but I am the tiger; it is a fire which consumes me, but I am the fire.

:::: debris

Because the historians chronicle how, when my brother Androgeos began to collect all the prizes at the Panathenaic games, King Aegeus commanded him to fight his most fearsome bull.

How brave bewildered Androgeos was gored and died on the stadium floor within minutes of entering.

:::: bradley manning song

Because it was not until I was in Iraq and reading secret military reports on a daily basis that I started to question the morality of what we were doing. This is why I turned over the files to which I had access to WikiLeaks, which made them public. I understand that my actions violated the law. I regret that my actions hurt anyone or harmed the United States. It was never my intent to hurt anyone. I only wanted to help people.

KIKI PETROSINO

Doubloon Oath

By dead gal or stove bones
by rainbow or red bird
red bird or cracked spine

by silk wrap or jaw jaw
by cold bodice, blush wing
tick tick or sunk ship
by tipped arrow, glass bite
by weird catch or *take that*
by chopped mountain, slick house
boatneck or gloss hog
striped awning, gold lawn
by *what's that* or *so much*
without me or full prof
full prof or nunchucks
blood orange, brain gob
time kill or toy star
by black doll or briar thorn
beg beg or gewgaw
by sweetmeat, or gunlock
or old maid or dreadnought
by weakness or whitecap
or grief-bacon, worksong
by fieldwork or field mix
slagged field or steel kilt
by bone-bruise or kneesock
I get my gift.

JESSY RANDALL

Museum Maps

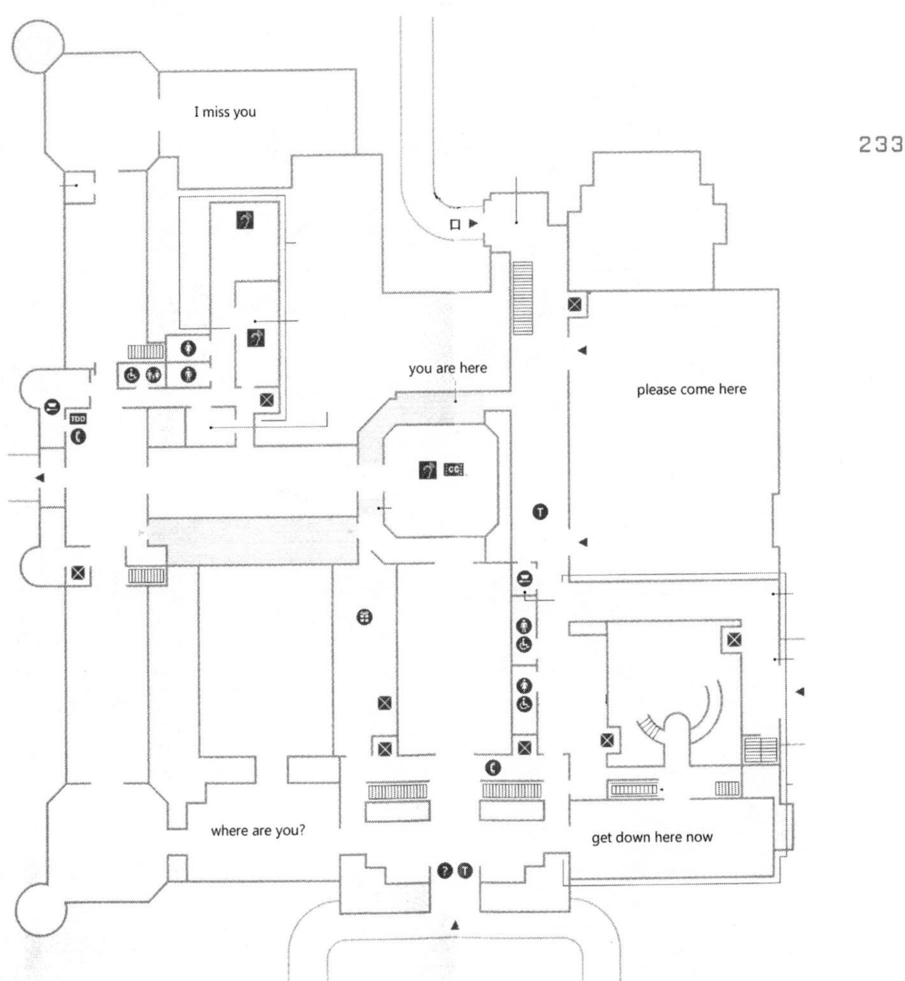

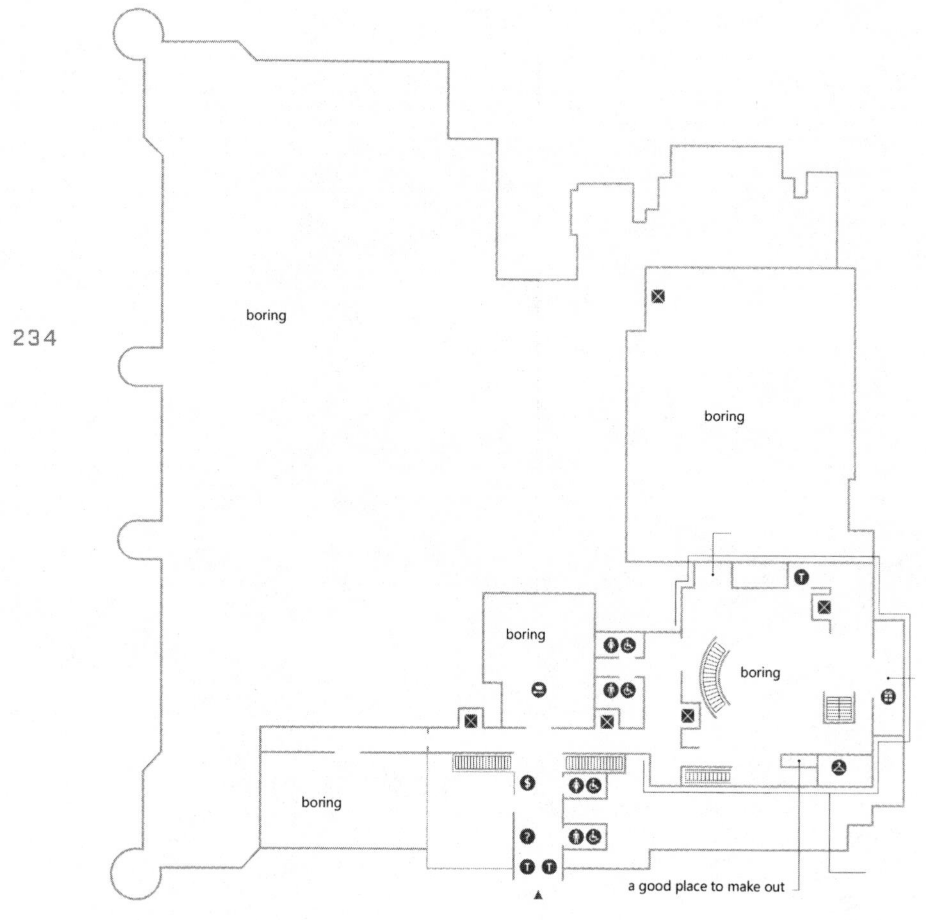
boring
boring
boring
boring
boring
a good place to make out

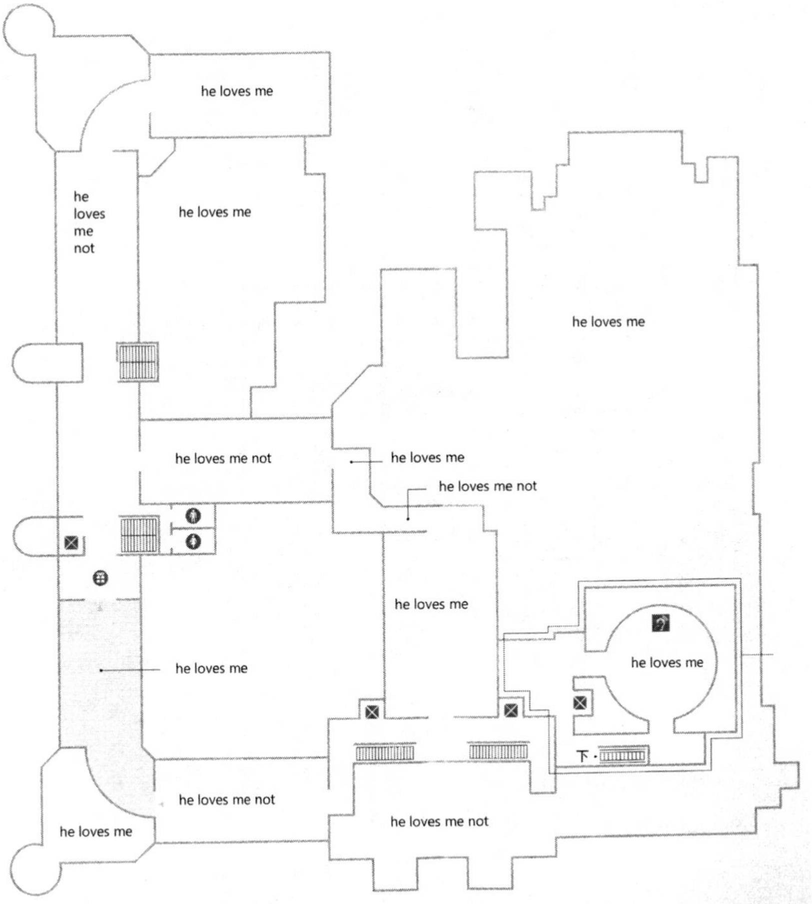

he loves me

he
loves
me
not

he loves me

he loves me

he loves me not

he loves me

he loves me not

he loves me

he loves me

he loves me

下

he loves me not

he loves me

he loves me not

Dominoes

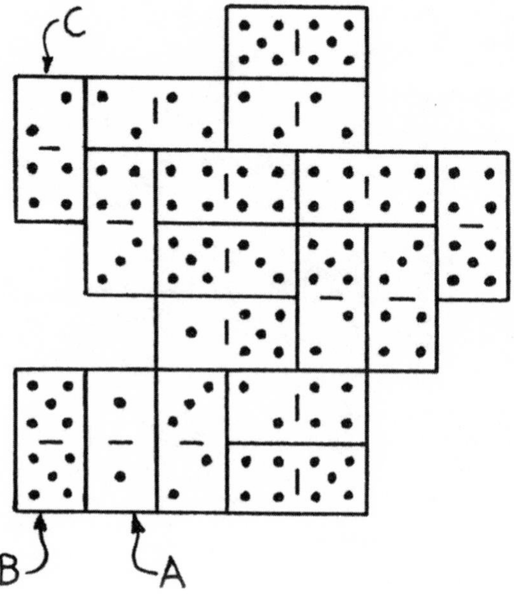

At the End of the Fifth Round

A. It's best to be first if you don't know what you're doing. They'll forgive your mistakes because you went first.

B. I don't like to be alone.

C. I wish I could get away from the endless counting and calculating. If I could just hold still for a moment, I know I'd feel all right.

JACOB REBER

Deep Sea Divers and Whaleboats

The stage is open water. The audience might be on rafts or wearing lifejackets. They will be wearing lifejackets and floating, wearing goggles.

In the openness floats a few boats, possibly real, possibly imaginary. Below the water are three divers. They stay under until they run out of air, then surface.

Curtain.

Camera and Knife

There is a film crew: the camera operator, the focus puller, the clapperloader, the boom operator, the lighting technician, and a negative cutter smoking a cigarette.

The director walks on stage. He pulls a razorblade from his pocket and walks off the stage, out into the audience. The film begins rolling.

The director cuts a member of the audience. The negative cutter already called for an ambulance. The film crew records the entire trip to the hospital, and the procedure that follows.

Curtain.

J D SCOTT

Cantica

🔥🔥🔥🔥🔥🔥🔥🔥🔥🔥🔥🔥🔥👬🔥🔥🔥🔥🔥🔥🔥🔥🔥🔥🔥🔥🔥

Locked in palm @ Inferno Ground Zero   Matty S is my donor

We on our way to a Halloween kegger

past Purgatorio

hand-in-hand   hard to arm

We in a limo   We on a cream horse   Or in Abercrombie & Fitch

Violencing each other w/ a battalion of cologne   And   We laugh

When I am good   Which I am inherently   He asks me a riddle

When I answer that riddle correctly I am given a magical thimble

to have a face touched by Matty S is to feel "futurist"

& "eternity"   No "dead ball" or "coffin corner"

Matty w/ those twinky pitaya lips

Matty w/ cherry thirst for jungle juice   Him

in a velveteen tracksuit w/ cyborg visor

Wires dangling out of his ~~scarecrow~~ socket

He is so flannelpunk My wilderness robot

(as if touch = ownership)

Yet still I touch

& I would not give him up for all the tina in Casper

Yes we ghosting We eidola We so kelpie so far above the drown

We rail in the biomechatronic High into the machine & scowl

@ all the angels outside of Eden Which Matty doesn't observe

(as those of nevermud cannot dream of that final return to dust)

Ribless & Samhain-bound We endure

& jaunt past the top song It goes like

♬ *O it's much to easy to scaffold someone else's corpse as yr muse*

& to hold someone else's hand out of obligation > compassion ♬

But those are concerns of the dead & the loveless & we worry not of the catafalque

Us the hyperalive

I love

I love his uneven eyes Those peepers of charity

glassed w/ a Y2K end zone

My droog My cumbrother Matty S

to black milk is to bask in the syzygy of shadow on shadow on shadow

& there is nothing to be gained by standing in the shadows w/ a golf club

and beating the pink goo out the heteroseraph   Not *a* hetero

The

The same

Gosh   to be shoulder pads   & absorb shock

& progress   & progress

O that sad   obliterated face   O youthful struggle

O infantalized Peter Pan fandom   O bambino rife w/ oratorio

When I want to let go of that fingersong   I don't

When I want to give in to the sacrifice   I magnanimous

When I hurt   I hold his digits harder   I diamond

No lookback for me   hehe

O my amber plains pop   O balladeer in blonde & blonde &

my charming Orpheus dumpster   My doppelgänger

What is the opposite of a necropolis   because I am there

w/ Matty S   We in a locker room @ the Pyramid of Giza

& Boston Market still holding hands   & a cathedral

made of sea glass & jute & still we hold hands

We grotesque & contaminate in Sears sweater catalogs

We netherworld & side-eye Lot's Wife

We who pass the Sweet Teen Room & bitter & umami

We @ Limelight (Alig's Drano® protégés) We who curl & chant

& continue & mirror ball

w/ our white sashimi skin so media pure Snowbabies™

nillas on mountain tops like a space of virtuality

This second life We MMOccult

like fetus as data in the horizon of canopic

(a sky burial vending machine where organs are stored in aluminum cylinders)

I am dressed as six six six ... & conjoin ... I beast

to razzia & echelon for Matty ... is to beget ... I pause

Outside of the pearls of St. Peter w/ Matty S I think

Ugh This is the struggle to hold hands 4eva

& passado Those Who Embalm We arrive

on Frat Row where jack-o'-lanterns spell

soft sentences to lime & to lick salt is to Matty S

& mezcal shot out of my magical thimble

& declare "climax!" Like this is shiver

This is the glory of the hart Not *a* glory The MacGuffin

we came for bound by friction ridges

of skin

We antler We stag-

ger We who agave and desert

We who odyssey & manna into six columns, six revolves, six Greek chambers

We who weapon in the topmost atrium

O heart!

We who do not bargain

or negotiate 

We pillar We ascend We aubade

We blitzkrieg We exit We conquer

We murmur We vibrate We summon

We Harlequin We Columbine We dove-of-peace

We tug-of-war We overcome We paradise

EVIE SHOCKLEY

fukushima blues

i've	wanted	long	*come*	well	now
long	to	time	*see*	i	i
heard	see	tokyo's	*japan*	thought	see
tokyo	japan	been	*someday*	it	japan
calling	someday	calling		was	is
		my		too	right
		name		great	around
				a	the
				distance	way

i	that	i	and	but	and
didn't	tsunami	never	her	the	i'm
feel	wave	felt	tsunami	aftershocks	drowning
the	didn't	the	wave	are	in
earthquake	even	earth's	didn't	still	them,
	touch	super	get	quiet-	lord
	my	shimmy	nowhere	coming	knows
	toes		near		
			my		
			toes		

i've
long
heard
tokyo
calling

a
distant
voice
from
a
distant
shore

so
long
i've
heard
tokyo
calling

but
never
made
it
to
that
distant
shore

so
the
earthquake
shook
loose
a
piece

and
the
tsunami
dragged
it
right
up
to
my
door

the
quake
shut
down
the
fukushima
party

and
the
tsunami
took
out
the
trash

the
quake
shut
down
fukushima
the
hard
way

and
the
tsunami
took
care
of
the
trash

i'm
not
sure
where
all
the
junk
got
dumped

but
i
heard
that
it
made
quite
a
splash

a
ghost
ship
sailed
itself
over
here

surrounded
by
all
kinds
of
debris

a
crewless
ship
haunted
its
way
across
the
pacific

along
with
autos,
unmarked
barrels,
and
all
kind
of
debris

shit's
washing
up
all
along
the
left
coast

loud
with
high-
volume
radio-
activity

i
remember
when
i
was
scared
to
try
sushi

but
once
i
did
i
was
hooked

yeah
i
used
to
be
squeamish
about
sushi

but
the
first
bite
got
me
hooked

now
i'm
an
asian
fusion
junkie

but
i
don't
want
the
tuna
in
my
sushi
cooked

we
laid
a
little
egg
of
cesium-
137

on
hiroshima
in
1945

we
laid
another
egg
of
cesium-
137—
a
fat
one—

on
nagasaki
back
in
'45

boy,
those
eggs
hatched
like
they
were
supposed
to

and,
man
oh
man,
has
the
species
multiplied . . .

BALTHAZAR SIMÕES

[Dear Emiel]

247

Dear Emiel,

I'm going to do a little experiment on you. I hope you don't mind. If you reject being used in my experiment you should stop reading right now! If you are still reading, you are a brave man! I like you, Emiel!

So, I'm going to try to hypnotize you. I've never done this before, but what harm is there in a little mesmerism? Maybe I'll become a mail order mesmerist. It's a little dream of mine. Are you ready, Emiel? Take out the polaroid I've enclosed.

Now, take a deep breath and stare into the stripes. Stare into the stripes, Emiel. Yes, just like that. You're really good at this!

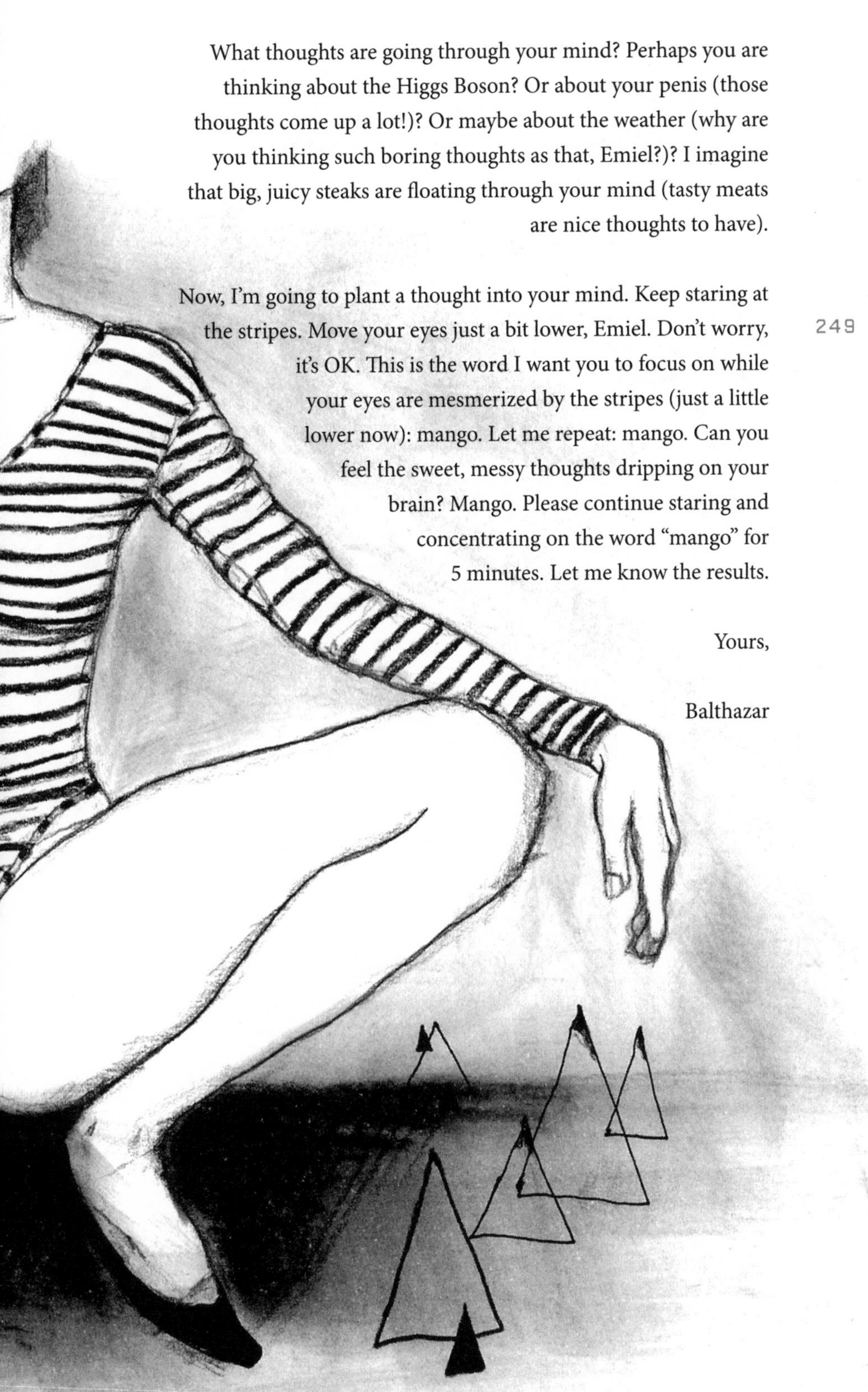

What thoughts are going through your mind? Perhaps you are thinking about the Higgs Boson? Or about your penis (those thoughts come up a lot!)? Or maybe about the weather (why are you thinking such boring thoughts as that, Emiel?)? I imagine that big, juicy steaks are floating through your mind (tasty meats are nice thoughts to have).

Now, I'm going to plant a thought into your mind. Keep staring at the stripes. Move your eyes just a bit lower, Emiel. Don't worry, it's OK. This is the word I want you to focus on while your eyes are mesmerized by the stripes (just a little lower now): mango. Let me repeat: mango. Can you feel the sweet, messy thoughts dripping on your brain? Mango. Please continue staring and concentrating on the word "mango" for 5 minutes. Let me know the results.

Yours,

Balthazar

GIOVANNI SINGLETON

illustrated equation no. 1

something about a look . . .   something about seeing . . .

don't   shoot

BRIAN KIM STEFANS

from *Mediation in Steam*

THIS, FINALLY, MY book
of philosophy
recollections, discouragements, *lex*
often reading circus
for humid terms
suspended in the wild percentage, moving
like cloud spots, frictions
of leg against leg
the music
this frantically the look
of seemingly improper moments, for the
book
protects, and then there's abundance
to elevate
the mundane, to its
synaesthetic upper station
where white funk makes its play, for
emotion, pleasure, pain, simple
it seems—to the roving challenger
bored, quite frankly, of this

* * *

ONE OF THE great english voices
cut
up, three stories
robert wyatt
hum, incredibly danceable
now, to the new knowledge
accrued with friendship

such self-referential grease
provokes the dim readership

in a vial of kittens, ribboning

what one considers meters rather
didactically
uncovers a gem

NAT SUFRIN

Now, Now Rahm Emanuel

None of
those people
be the people.
They offer
no secrets
no big treats
no mood slings.
Not a peep
from the sun today
but be happy:
the new mayor
is a dancer.
I call him
up I say
Rahm fuck
you he says
Nat fuck
you we salivate
for hours over
the promise
of daggering:
the brand
new you
too dancehall.
Now under
this now now
we can now
know now.
Sometime earlier

today we will
feel ok when
damn how
especially if.

VINCENT TORO

MicroGod Schism Song

Robot pilgrim colonic. Illicit volt rot.

  Motor imp. Six digit pin prick.

Sonic broom. Scoop fool's gold from

  slipshod mind pod. Pick locks

of COBOL roosts. Phototrophic bliss,

  Phonic distortion. Tin foil trolls

in Wifi torpor. Oblong X Box flips

  ribs into port prisons or sim

forts. Iris lit with Nook prisms. Whip two

  million gig pistil. Piston shift

from groin to droid rods. Zip witch or whiz

  kid. Proto-Snob incision. Toxic

pools of blown skin trips. Thin Fission

  of word from window. Mint

condition solipsism. Ion soot loops. Bit coin

  cops kiss in Biochip grid lock.

Nitric worm hollow. Info mortis.

Binary Fusion Crab Canon

I O
LI OC
ILI CRO
IILI CRFO
ITLII ERFCO
IYILTI CFOAER
IYTIILNROETACF
TLIIYFAENTCIOR
LOEYRTTAICFNII
NRITCIALTOEYIF
RNOEACFLTYTIII
YRILICIONAETFT
AEIIIOYLTTRCFN
AEIIIOYCFLNRTT
ACEFIIILNORTTY
YETILTOCARIFIN
FREATICLIONITY
LITACIT INREYOF
REACTION FILITY
INTRICATE LIFE O Y
I LEARN Y I COT FIT
I C FINITE ROYAL T
Y C I L T R E A I F N O T I
I C L E A N I F I T R Y T O
L T R Y I A E I I C F N T O
Y T I L A E R N O I T C I F
I L A T R E Y C I T I N O F
T E A R I L Y F O N C I T I
YE IL RAT COIN FIT
LITE RAY FON T CIN
REAL YIT I C NO FIT
REALITY FICTION
RITE A LY TO F I N I C
RALI YET TINI FOC
LIT YEAR F I T I C O N
Y ART LIE C O F T I N I
E A T L I R Y N O T I F I C
Y T I L A E R N O I T C I F
Y I FEL TO C I I N ART
I C TOY LIFE IN ART
TIL I C YIN OR FATE
Y CANT I RIOT LIFE
TITLE YO RICAN IF
FEAR IN COY TITIL
COY RAT FINITE LI
TO RAIN FELICITY
Y TEL IT FOR I CAN
FREACTIONILITY
TIONFREACTILIY
CATFORITYINEIL
3AT6ORITY9N59L
3L996AORITY5TN
135699LORITYTN
135699NOL9050R
10360599595748
00134555678999
13569994005758
456990 490573
45699 49573
4560 5573
110 523
01 33
1 0

RODRIGO TOSCANO

from *Explosion Rocks Springfield*

The Friday evening gas explosion in Springfield
leveled a strip club next to a day care.

"Bleed it here, the gas—watch.
Gauge zero's—see, both ends.
Cinch it—there, till it pools.
Gauge should read 25.
Double tap it, why not.
Eight, has to be eight feet
O2 tanks and this one
Or five foot wall between.
Now, that's premise regs, right?
C.O.'s have their *own* regs.
Zone, each one has its reg.
Same principal, you'll see.
Double strap it, always.
These trucks, they shake, awful.
Brewskies at The Bouillon?
Nah. Stick a fork in me
This shift always, I'm cooked.
Thursday—right, at the hall.
You should chair it, why not?
All right, buddy, be safe.
Don't let them gals fleece you."

The Friday evening gas explosion in Springfield leveled a strip club next to a day care.

"Unbutton here, this strap.
Even jugs, see, real nice.
Now clip on this red tail
One minute into it.
Double flare it, why not.

Five, can only be five
Per booth—including you.
Or eight, if two of you.
Now, that's this club's reg, right?
Other clubs make their own.
Boss, each has a "vision."
Same old dance, count on it.
Well, maybe *two* buttons.
These strobes, they blind, crazy.
Night owl shots at The Coop?
Nah. Scoop me on a cone
This shift always, I'm licked.
Thursday—right, at my house.
You should chair it, why not?
All right, honey, be safe.
Don't let them guys steer you."

The Friday evening gas explosion in Springfield leveled a strip club next to a day care.

"Spread out the ice like this.
Twelve chocolate, three white milks.
Watch how I wedge them in.
Roster should say fifteen.
Do a roll call, why not.
Four, only four can go
This bathroom and that one.
That's *this* center's regs, right?
Other ones have their own.
Counties, each one decides.
Similar norms, you'll see.
Yeah, check for leaky ones
These cartons, they rip, tons.
Rump shake shooters at Ski's?
Nah. Crunk on without me
This shift always, I'm zonked.
Thursday—right, at the rec.
You should chair it, why not?
All right then girl, be safe.
Don't let these kids crank you."

The Friday evening gas explosion in Springfield leveled a strip club next to a day care.

Spartacus sprinklers (top rail)
Serial no. 21809A
Inspector 480F
Jiangxi Quality Products
Night Hawk Importers, San Bruno, CA

Roman Roads Distributors, Phoenix, AZ
Port of entry, Tacoma, WA
Tankard 10179.03
Inspector 4201
ILO quarterly report:
Case study 1142
Tingting Liu, 23, female
I.D. 41732
Platform 12, line 8, station 4
Muscular skeletal paralysis
3rd metatarsal taped to 2nd phalangeal
4th proximal splinted to 5th distal
OSHA Region 1 final report:
Incident 2267, explosion (gas)
Inspector 505F
Sprinklers inoperable
Logic Tree branch 20
System of Safety failure
Mitigation device
16 drill holes stoppered
Weld burs not filed
Citation: 29CFR.1910.159(c)(12)
Notes: inspector 505F on leave
DOL budget sequestered
PUB.L. 112-25
District 2, 112th Congress
United States of America

The Friday evening gas explosion in Springfield leveled a strip club next to a day care.

Spartacus Sprinklers (top rail)
Serial no. 21809A
Scrap metal yard F-2
Stripped steel tankard 28
Sampson Recyclers Ltd., Pittsfield, MA
Steelworkers local 4-12026
Smelting furnace 48
Slab beam rollout batch 81.2014
Semper Fortis Steel Precision Corp, Brooklyn, NY
Steelworkers local 4-200
Section cutting station no. 12
Steel cylinder hollow type 2b
Store & send department 4
Spirit of 76 Commercial Furnishing Corp, Slidell, LA
Steelworkers local 3-275
Sargon Sprinklers (bottom rail)
Serial no. 321911B
Sink coating station 12
Sanding unit 25
Seal testing station no. 7
Sprinklers standard specification 29CFR1910.159(b)
Station inspector 13
Sales packaging room H
Sort and storage garage 4
Second incidence of forklift crushing worker's toes
Spirit of 76 Personnel Motivation Free Cupcake Fridays director, Chet Baker
Steelworkers local 3-275 chief steward, Marynella Fernandez
Section 5, clause 2 "Management shall comply with all state and federal standards"
Safety committee grievance no. 78: unannounced station rotations / inadequate training
Staff training regulation arbitration hearing 501.P.36
Sargon Sprinklers 1st annual wet t-shirt contest
Super Sonic Dance Club, 3rd Floor, Picayune, MS

The Friday evening gas explosion in Springfield
leveled a strip club next to a day care.

I remember the breeze right before . . .
Burs of—was it willow—slant-falling.
The gray sidewalk, schist granules, scattering.
A brown dumpster lid smushing its green plastic, sandwich meat.
A rat made its debut, but for a moment.

I remember an awning string's knotted tip soft-thudding a windowpane
—tympani's uneven beat.
The rustle of stray trash—bass strings, almost rising
—but never.
And the chopper, the chopper—spittletatootling, spittletatootling—
A proud boot landing on obedient asphalt.
The stern, uncrying chrome.
The flighty flames decorative gas tank.

I can't forget the beryllium blue sunshades
—orange hued at a glance.
And the stars and bars, starched, pressed, bandana.
Nation Idol Gorge
But for a moment
Then
Boom.

The Friday evening gas explosion in Springfield leveled a strip club next to a day care.

I remember the plume right after . . .
Orbs of—was it cinnamon—black-rising.
Vapor gray whitening shingle powder rain.
A dumpster lid sheered off a gravestone's angel face.
A hawk's claws claimed the stump.

I remember two spouts of thin flame, blue, making an X
—mind's waking dream.
The hissing of gurgling plastic, supplicant—sick
—stomach's inner eyeball.
And the bathtub, the bathtub—sittin' pretty—sittin' pretty—
The hysteric roof flopping on an unfazed floor.
The wise, ever-wakeful steel beams.
The cheery glass—beaming—everywhere.

I can't forget that purple doorknob
—horny at a glance.
And the plump couch stuffing foam, blazing, angry.
City's Final Chorus
But for a moment
Then
Shsh.

The Friday evening gas explosion in Springfield
leveled a strip club next to a day care.

I don't remember the very moment . . .
Flashes of—was I daydreaming—Biloxi Bound.
The termite swarm at dusk, balling up, sprinkling.
A skeeter swirling in its hotel pool—for the first time.
A no-see-um bug popped out from nowhere—but for a moment—to romp.

I can't say I recall Cleopatra's hairpiece flying off in a speeding four-cylinder
  vehicle
—Empire of the Great Somewhere, but never.
And the flying fish, the flying fish—hither-flopping, hither-flopping—
The carefree palms, twerking, injured.
The bald, unyielding sun, giddy.
Tentative feet in knee high water, gripping.

Have I forgotten the name of that triple IPA—something like
—Rondez The Moon à la Batshit.
And the ample sized black pockadots—in my eyes, twerking, carefully.
Empire of the Great Somewhere
But for a moment
Then
Then

TOM TRUDGEON

Part 2/ 21/ 6 from *Study for 14 Pieces for Charles Curtis*

A.| The balance on which impressions are weighed is not the
impression of a balance.
1./ There is no criterion for correctness
2./ Fragmentary assemblance
3./ *and* common language
a.| it is everyone who speaks when no one else is present.
b.| now, particular door

B.| emission of inarticulate sound
1./ resolve
2./ as *having been buried*
a.| sometimes the pastoral
b.| let us imagine a table.

C.| Seemingly indifferent w/o use of apparatus
1.1/ unverified relation
1.2/ referential to that known only.
a.| from the object—its membrane.

C1.| What use of sentence is thought of?
1./ it is in addition, a representation
a.| as it can't be for anyone else
b.| transferal-ideas to stones; plants.

D.| *dead transition*
1./ but I in my hand.

SARAH VAP

[13 untitled poems]

Where there is no love, put love—and you will find love. —John of the Cross

Where there is no love, put love—and you will find love. Where there is no memory, put memory— and you will find memory. Where there is no pull, put iron filings, put metals, put bindings, put jaw traps wide open, and there you will find pull. —John of the Cross

Where there is no speculation, put inflation—and you will find love's victim. Put the victim. Put the operation. Put operations all across the victim. Put very quiet calls for each other. If I understand, what we want here is an increase. —John of the Cross

Where there is no cannibalization, put wire—and you will find wire. Where there is no cannibalization, put memory—and you will find mind. Where there is no wire halo, put wire wrapped tightly around a mind. Put wire wrapped tightly around a torso. Put wire tightly wrapped around many bodies at the same time. Where there are no saints, put cannibalization—put a body—and there you will find even more. —John of the Cross

Untenable? Where there is no love, put continuation or put increase or put proliferation—and there you will find the love untenable. Language is not infinity. Language is not hopeful. There is no rapture in language. I admit that I had hoped to "love" and "be loved." —John of the Cross

The actual bear is in a skirt. The actual bull is a saint. The actual fish is a multibillion-dollar industry. The actual skirt is a fundamental. What do you secretly believe in? What do you secretly want? Me—if I could conceive, I could increase. —John of the Cross

But where are the animals of actual praise. Where are the animals of actual mercy. Where is the coin in the animal, in the infant animal? —John of the Cross

Where there is no goodwill, put acquisition. Put incessant proprietary technology. Where there is no goodwill, put cannibalization. Put host. Put incarnation. Put transmutation. Where there is no love, put abstract animals. Where there is no love, put lipstick. Put mascara. Put lipstick down the rat. Hairspray into the nose of the rat. Where there is no love, put lipstick on abstract animals. —John of the Cross

Where there is no infant, put Americium—there you will find the infant radiating. —John of the Cross

A bear's body is a list of hard facts about her body. A bull's body is a list of hard facts about her body. A man's body is a list of hard facts about her body. A man's body should outperform its competition. —John of the Cross

Where there is void, there you will find the Index. There you will find relentlessness. There you will proliferate. But was that a void to be filled? That was not a void to be filled. Did you think that was a void to be filled? Is this what the Index told you? —John of the Cross

Where there is no love. Where there is no love. Where there are no super-angels. Where there is no blast wave. Where there is no cooling pool. Where there is no half-life. Where there is no trash-fish. Where there is no by-catch. Where there is no inedible or infant species of fish. Where there is no love. Where there is no curve. Where there is no Index. Where there is no woman. Where there is no price. Where there is no infant. Where there is no price. Where there is no animal. —John of the Cross

Index, put actual bears, put actual bulls, put actual cows, put actual lipstick on the actual animals of real earth. —John of the Cross

DIVYA VICTOR

Color: A Sequence of Unbearable Happenings

> *The story reveals the meaning of what otherwise would remain an unbearable sequence of sheer happenings.*
> — Hannah Arendt, *Men in Dark Times*

1

It was a nice try. It was a nice move that made the black move to white. A nice move that turned most things away from what they were looking at. Sometimes the way they moved suggested something other than the color of the objects that they looked at. Sometimes these colors turned to ash and then to dust and then they walked away from those colors. In a nice way the walk away had a melody closer to silence than anything else. More than anything it possessed a kind of slow and somber hum. White and blanched like poached eggs in a cream bowl. Slumbering fetal pups overcome by a bitch's thick milk. So much of your eyes are waiting to sup on the right teat. So much of color is waiting. So much of color is in the wait to be seen. One thing radiating points to the other that is not lit.

2

One thing radiating is in the middle of shade. The shade of the light is uniform and issued to the newly fleshed. To take issue with the midriff of a shade is to force air into a similar stillness. A surplus of inexpensive sky. An expanse of twill which mentions the hands. A flesh of color is the willful opening to some other gesture before a body walks up to you in a warm alley. It is the surface to which the name arrives in the eye. The eye in question is at a wake. A flesh is a survey of other black objects coated with lacquer daubed with plaster plumped by upholstery hoisted plum in a sulking roasted sow's mouth. This color is a sullied mutton or a beef with someone who owns another name blurred by matted voices calling them into recognition. This is something walking up to you with a face of apology or greeting or wearing or dying in a borrowed trench.

3

As specific as something appearing in a borrowed trench sits longer unobserved at a wake. A length of invisibility turns into a bruise the closer it gets to a fist. Indivisible into parts yet invited to take part, a waiting body is a puddle forming inside a coat. Swollen like knuckles like red but not red-orange or dark red or plummy blood pudding, which are shades of a similar livid lineage. The lineage forms in someone's drowsy wait near bystanders when the dark will break in two. It breaks into indefinite distances of abrupt brightness we call mornings. This body's color is a startling sleep hung on a hammock between two points: one known and the other less known. There is an occurrence of pigment and it suggests a history growing in sand or a method of preparing lakes or the pliant application of arms to a row. This body faces you with a knot of a face made of alum or lye and wet with linseed oils. That body is folding a glance into a fist sized thing to be pocketed by a bystander. Collecting the toe collecting the finger nail the hanging thing cooling, by the by. Walking away from this means something about solving water into fog. To be waded through and not whetted by. To see color is to apply yourself to a stone like a barber's blade. With a certain lilt of the neck. A pile of tools and all the lashes in a lather at this wake for someone's body. A bloom of raspberries wilting in a tureen once used for serving offal soup.

4

A bloom of raspberries made an example when for instance a stick touches a hand, when for instance the water turns to a boil and the boil turns back to the water with a questioning glance. Some examples of instances that are taken when something is not self evident like a hanging thing cooling or a rhubarb pie huddling into the corner of a meshed cupboard. This body's color is an instance of an example where for instance the act of bringing the witness to the witness stand where the witness sits instead. This is a confusing proposition of verbs fat with a pleasant symmetry at court. A court takes as evidence the small flush of violet that grows transparent after the second stoning when blood ribbons away from the body. Where the blood pools the body blushes fuchsia then dusky plum draining from an eggy ochre. Its sleep is a growing bruise in the ground. In moderation the cause of color is a disagreement between two similarities. In its basic form the cause of color is the tooth left behind at the curb. Fusing someone and something color emerges as a better forgery of resemblance limp and livid at once. Someone is always begging you not to confound small bits of egg whites with other white bodies swilling back and forth like irascible pebbles at the bottom of any water.

5

Someone is always begging you not to shelve this thing at the helm of being named. On the verge it is something flagged on a pole and striped with strips of flesh waving or hanging or a pair of feet not touching the ground when it ought not to do otherwise. Flagged as otherwise color is a swarm of desire formed while waiting too long in a crowd. Wading far enough in the shallow of pigment as if a wavelet of a person has its eventual place against a rock or a shore or a dock of an assembly. An assembly is a gathering that can carry a body through its due process to an end. To carry a body to its becoming as carrion by suspending the weight of a person as strange fruit for the crows to pluck. To carry on as if color is an area of skin hoisted by a glance or carried like a chip on the shoulder of mutton. To carry on as if this does not drown you in weals and welts or turn your chest into a whistle or a willowy hollow blowing whist whist whist go away.

KIM VODICKA

Unisex One-Seat♥r

I get new ponders each time Michelangelos.

I get new geniuses each time Albert Einsteins.

Beethoven right between the eyes.

Drunk thought, best thought.

I entertain suicide like a party guest
and drink my whiskey with dirt.

I've a junkie with your name on it.

I've a cross-eyed bitch with your name on it.

I'd gone to the lithe before you'd come ovum.

For I am a kite
and die
and key to thy heart
divine.

I wipe my ass with Swarovski crystals.

I wipe my ass with fine violence.

I shook your hand and I felt
GOD DAMN.

The thou that I throw unnamed flowers upon,
I throw unnamed tampons upon,
I throw bloody.

Inoculate me, baby,
I'm so so sore
in the afternew.

Put your dick in edgewise,
like a word in.

My tongue,
a red carpet
rolled out
for your gods
to trickle down
to whatever
that dangly thing
in the back
of the throat
is called—
the uvula—
the target
you aim for
when you blow it.

When cock
is of
the essence.

And then ALL OF A SUDDEN,
these ass and this tits,
and we were more bored than ever.

If I ever thought, maybe,
iffin I ever thought a'tall,
then perhaps, perchance,
I'd find the words to speak,
the speakeasy to vomit up
fine worlds of meth
and throw off the challenge
with a machine gun.

If I had it to do over,
I'd swallow it inch for inch.

I'd fuck a femur.

I'd stick my fag in it.

I'd come on the face on the milk carton.

I'd break a glass in the heat of my shimmy.

I'd grind my shit on your shit

for
nothing.

Just trying to get my finger into the pot of dingers.

I'll bet you say that to any old divine.

Now, if you'd excuse me,
I have to go repo some dirt.

Notice

Catherine Wagner is a content provider who has been requested by David Boeving to deliver a work of poetry to be published in *Bathhouse. Bathhouse* and David Boeving will not compensate Wagner monetarily for her labor; however, as poetry production is assessed as "research" at the institution where she works, and because 33.3% of her time on the job is meant to be spent on research, it is possible to estimate that she will be paid $31.00 by Miami University for writing the present text. Of the various solicits for content provision she has received in recent years, only the Poetry Foundation, an organization endowed by the Lilly pharmaceutical fortune, has offered monetary compensation for content generated by Wagner. Other arts-media organizations, lacking or rejecting similar resources, process content through a set of vectors that is sometimes described as a gift economy, sometimes as a source of symbolic capital. These vectors move through the bodies of content providers, editors, interns, and other workers, through the paper-producing trees, money jobs, living rooms, office photocopiers, government agencies, inherited funds and power plants that enable the processing of poetry in the marketplace. In a bid to use the percentage of her body and time occupied by these vectors more efficiently, and to buff their surface areas to an agreeable or disagreeable shine, Wagner is currently responding to solicits for work with this text being processed by you. Wagner would like to express gratitude here and now for your time and for the work you do.

TYRONE WILLIAMS

Coterie Chair

the music, having not yet rested . . .

Once upon a first, two pursue
one another around a third, the throne
of abbreviated extensions however throng
threat. Both, pursued by each other's
wake, taken for a gathering storm,
jack-and-jill-o'-lanterns (as-is lamps
nee decapitated—poles. The drag
queen effect circulates as butch
capital—circumcises prosthetic apps:
boo! [nee book], says the step up,
step down, an Escheresque Zeno-
sum from top from bottom, closet to close-up,
where a wide sashay is said to segue
yo-yo style: hip-hop hip-drop.

RONALDO V. WILSON

Lucy, Finally

I'm sitting here, looking at a shadow, on a wall, looking at a bug, sealed beneath
    the shower curtain,
sitting next to a radiator, burning close.

I'm sitting next to being ignored, as I try to etch out my age,
the light crags flirting with my face.

I'm sitting next to the space in which I am occupying space, where my heart is
    no longer snagged.
I'm sitting next to the wall, where I am engaged.

where I am looking in a mirror, hear the sneeze rings, and I'm feeling kind
    of iffy,
and what I realize is that I do not like the way that another

who is like me, an object, lit by the light of the morning, looks over my
    shoulder.
There is one of us, a buffed in black, a white short-sleeved in the forest,

who is walking through an entrenched notion, dumb. I have a surface. I have
    a spine.
Too, I have a way of being out of which my body springs through the walls.

"I can't help you."—"Sorry don't touch this."—Sorry the night is complicated,
    even
in the way I run, too—the cardio blast up the hill, says, "You, too, can look
    like this."

STEVEN ZULTANSKI

from *Bribery*

If there's one thing that's certain for everyone, at all times, no matter where they live or what they obsess over

unreasonably, it's that one can't, at any given moment, get any worse than one already is, without sliding into another

moment altogether. Of course I'm already awful, but only as awful as I am right now, and just as one holds out hope for tomorrow, knowing it will be better than today, if only because, finally, today will be gone, I hope when I'm worse

I'll be better too: better, for example, the way women are better than men because they have to put up with men, like saints, while men go around giving the impression they're men, like assholes; better the way poor people

are better than rich people because they take what the rich people hand out to them, like monotonous jobs and fast food and jail time

and work-related bladder cancer; better the way non-white people are better than white people because they aren't allowed to write

the oppressive laws they live under or order the police into their neighborhoods to beat the shit out of their kids; better the way children are better than adults at being unable to fight back when their parents take out their failures on them; better the way whoever is being bombed right now by American planes is better than

the pilots of those planes because they're scattered in more pieces and cover more area; better the way every other person will always be better than me simply by being bigger than me, their thoughts and actions everywhere I'm not—and so on and so on, one thing is better than another forever, until you die. But for now, if I live even one more day—if this isn't the last time I taste water, sweat through my shirt, squint,

run my tongue over dry lips, find myself unable to speak, cover my eyes—then I won't escape a certain extra degree of dipshit eternity, I'll end up

giving myself at least one more thing to hate about myself, either by doing something I think I dislike, or by doing something I think other people dislike, like committing

some more crimes, which, like the laws they protect, are every- where at once, written down. There are plenty to choose from. For example, robbing a store at knifepoint.

I did that.

I pulled on a skeleton mask and went with two friends to a little bodega on Bleecker and 4th and we filmed ourselves pushing the clerk into the back room and basically

giving him a hard time and grabbing him around the belly and shaking him as if coins would fall out of his armpits. He was soft and scared and had no idea

we weren't there to hurt him; a few times he even laughed quietly (it sounded more like coughing) when we poked or pushed him, as if he were trying to get in on the joke and play along. At some point he tripped and almost

fell over, but I held him up by the arms while he steadied himself. For some reason I expected him to thank me,

which of course he didn't (because I was robbing him), and so I said *thank you* for him, to him, very softly, and he stared at the floor and coughed again, but it didn't sound like laughing anymore. We didn't take much money because there wasn't much to take and that was fine, we weren't really there for the money anyway, and I mostly regret propping the clerk back up, not because it would have been funny to see him fall —it might not have been—but because

letting him tumble would have been a small enough form of self-relinquishment to make me seem ridiculous

but not quite as terrible as I'd like, because I like to disappoint myself, to make myself sad. It feels good. It would have been

better if I had not only robbed the store and poked the clerk's gut but also pushed him over, if not on his face then at least on his knees, an even more humiliating and suppliant position; this

extra little flourish of cruelty might have granted me a sense of power over him that I would not have wanted and would have been too much for me, but instead I intuitively reconciled my crime to my *sense of self* by

doing something just a little bit nice, and not even nice in a way meant to facilitate the patient savoring of a greater cruelty, like buying a lover

dinner right before abandoning them in the street, but nice in a nice way—though I know the clerk didn't experience my gesture of kindness

in terms of kindness, which is a relief. And I can always do something worse, which is also a relief.

Acknowledgments

Will Alexander: I want to thank Janice Lee and *Entropy* for originally posting these writings.

Emily Anderson: The story "Silver" first appeared in *Conjunctions* 63, Speaking Volumes (Fall 2014).

Aaron Apps: "The Formation of This Grotesque Fatty Figure" appeared in *Passages North*, issue 36 (Spring 2015).

Dodie Bellamy: "Cunt Wordsworth" was previously published in *Cunt Norton* (Los Angeles: Les Figues, 2013).

Anselm Berrigan: a version of "rectangle 71" was originally published in *New American Writing* 32 (2014) under the title "rectangle 96."

Jeremy Blachman: "Rejected Submissions to *The Complete Baby Name Wizard*" was originally published in *The Shrug 3* (theNewerYork Press, 2013).

Shane Book: "Mack Daddy Manifesto" was first published in Shane Book's poetry collection *Congotronic* (University of Iowa Press/House of Anansi Press, 2014).

Rachel Cantor: "Everyone's a Poet," *Ninth Letter* 11, no. 1 (Spring/Summer 2014).

Xavier Cavazos: "Sanford, Florida" originally appeared in the chapbook *Barbarian at the Gate* (Poetry Society of America, 2014).

Ching-in Chen: "bhanu feeds soham a concession," *Verse Wisconsin* (April 2014), 113–14. Note: a monster response arranged by Ching-In Chen from Soham Patel's poem, "Poem for the Animals" and Bhanu Kapil's *Incubation: A Space for Monsters* (Leon Works, 2006).

Cecilia Corrigan: Many thanks to Lisa Robertson, Madeleine Plonsker, Joshua Corey, Davis Schneiderman, and Robert Archambeau at &Now Books. *Titanic* was produced in residence at Lake Forest College.

Santino Dela: I would like to thank Steve Roggenbuck and the Boost House team for the time and effort they put into *The Yolo Pages* anthology in which this work was originally published. I'd also like to thank everyone else, but I'm running out of time, so I will just thank you.

Darcie Dennigan: "The Ambidextrous" first appeared in *Thermos Mag*, March 26, 2014, https://thermosmag.wordpress.com.

Andrew Durbin: "You Are My Ducati" first appeared in *Triple Canopy* 19, It Speaks of Others.

Thomas Sayers Ellis: An excerpt from "Conspiracy Smile [A Poet's Guide to the Assassination of JFK and the Assassination of Poetry]" originally appeared in *The Baffler*. Reprinted by permission of the author.

Sesshu Foster: "Movie Version: Hell to Eternity" first appeared in *Párrafo* 6.

C. S. Giscombe: 4 and 5 from "Early Evening." The "Early Evening" sequence appeared in *Iowa Review* 44, no. 2 (Fall 2014).

Alexis Pauline Gumbs: "'Black Studies' and all its children" was published in issue 17 of *Eleven Eleven*.

Elizabeth Hall: From "I Have Devoted My Life to the Clitoris," *P-Queue*, Fall 2014.

Brecken Hancock: "The Art of Plumbing" from *Broom Broom* © Brecken Hancock, 2014. Used with the permission of Coach House Books.

Duriel Harris: "Simulacra: American Counting Rhyme" was originally published in *stereoTYPE*, edited by Sharon Arnold and C. Davida Ingram (Bridge Productions/LxWxH Publications, 2014).

Lilly Hoang and Giménez-Smith: This excerpt was originally published in *Big Lucks*.

Jill Jichetti: "TITLE! JILLWRITES CURATES MAPS!" first appeared in *Collected*, the journal of the graduating class of the Department of Writing of the School of the Art Institute of Chicago in 2014. The journal's theme was Maps.

Janine Joseph: "Between Chou and the Butterfly" first appeared in *The Journal* 38.2 (Spring 2014).

Bhanu Kapil: I would like to acknowledge the findings and teaching of Larissa Lai and Jen Hofer, who taught classes at Naropa as part of a job search process. I would like to acknowledge Juliana Spahr's talk and practicum that she gave as part of a symposium on Territory, also at the Jack Kerouac School of Disembodied Poetics. I would like to acknowledge the brilliant Naropa students of The Hybrid and also Experimental Prose who were part of the complex, improvised, and durational classroom space in which we incubated these questions individually, and as a group.

Aaron Kunin: "An Essay on Tickling" appeared in the web journal *Triple Canopy* (Fall 2014), and was later collected in the book *Cold Genius* (Fence, 2014).

Sophia Le Fraga: from *I RL, YOU RL*, previously published in *Troll Thread*.

Sueyeun Juliette Lee: "[G calls]" from *Juliette and the Boys* was first published as chaplet 158, "Juliette and the Boys" (Feb. 2014) printed by Belladonna*.

Dawn Lundy Martin: "Mo[dern] [Frame]" was previously published on the Ms. Magazine Blog, http://msmagazine.com/blog/2014/04/29/five-feminist-poems-for-national-poetry-month-5-modern-frame/, and in *Life in a Box is a Pretty Life* (Nightboat Books).

Joyelle McSweeney: The excerpt from *Dead Youth, or, the Leaks* first ran on Hyperallergic; *Dead Youth, or, The Leaks* was published in 2014 by Litmus Press.

Holly Melgard: "Alienated Labor" originally appeared in *Clausius App*, issue 6, 2014.

Tyler Mills: "H-Bomb" first appeared in the February 2014 issue of *Believer*.

elena minor: "rrs FEED" is from *TITULADA* (Noemi Press, 2014).

Nick Montfort: "Through the Park" was originally presented on the site Grand Text Auto and first appeared in print in *#!* (Counterpath Press, 2014).

Fred Moten: "harriot + harriott + sound +" was published in *The Enemy*, May 15, 2014.

Daniel Nadler: from "The Lacunae," Copyright © 2014 Conjunctions. From *Conjunctions* 63, Speaking Volumes (Fall/November 2014) Published by Bard College, edited by Bradford Morrow.

Kelly Nelson: "Inkling" first appeared, in part, in *Found Poetry Review*, vol. 8.

Mendi + Keith Obadike: "The Wash House" was originally published in *Big House / Disclosure* (1913 Press, 2014). The book documents our intermedia suite of the same name commemorating the 200th anniversary of the British slave trade. The project is composed of a 200-hour-long sound installation, 200 text scores on rooms and relations in the big house, meditative lyrics, and graphic scores inspired by architecture and a writing system called nsibidi.

Kiki Petrosino: "Doubloon Oath" previously appeared in the *Los Angeles Review of Books*.

Jessy Randall: The three maps first appeared in *M58* in October 2014 as

Museum Maps: You Are Here, He Loves Me, and Makeout. The map illustrations are taken from the Korean version of the 2011 brochure for the American Museum of Natural History in New York City.

Jacob Reber, "Deep Sea Divers and Whaleboats" and "Cameras and Knives" previously appeared in the January 2014 issue of *PANK* online.

Evie Shockley: "fukushima blues" first appeared in *Fence* (2014). Reprinted by permission of the author.

Balthazar Simões: "[Dear Emiel]" originally appeared in *The Shrug 3: Time* (tNY Press; formerly theNewerYork). Balthazar is thankful for mangoes and stripes. To clarify, *my* work is the textual piece. The illustration is by Meerweh (Nadine Kappacher).

Brian Kim Stefans, the two excerpts from "Mediation in Steam" first appeared in *Lana Turner* 7 (2014).

Vincent Toro: "MicroGod Schism Song" was first published in *Really System* Issue Four, Sell A Mystery (Fall 2014).

Rodrigo Toscano: the pieces from *Explosion Rocks Springfield* first appeared in *Tripwire* Magazine, no. 7 (2014).

Tom Trudgeon: "Part 2/ 21/ 6 from *Study for 14 Pieces for Charles Curtis*" was first published in *Out of Nothing* 7 (Dec. 12, 2013). It was originally titled "Part 2; 21/6—Selections from *Study for 14 Pieces for Charles Curtis*."

Sarah Vap: [13 untitled poems] was originally published in *The Journal* 38.4 (Fall 2014). It will be included in *Viability*, a collection forthcoming from Penguin in fall 2015.

Kim Vodicka: "U n i s e x O n e – S e a t ♥ r" was originally published in *Smoking Glue Gun*, vol. 10, June 4, 2014.

Catherine Wagner" "Notice" was published in *Bathhouse* 11.2 (Spring 2014).

Tyrone Williams: "Coterie Chair" was previously published in *Out of Nothing* 7 (Jan. 2014).

Steven Zultanski: An excerpt from *Bribery*. Copyright 2014 Ugly Duckling Presse. Reprinted with permission of Ugly Duckling Presse.

Contributors

WILL ALEXANDER is a poet, novelist, playwright, philosopher, visual artist, and pianist. He is concerned with the meta-dimensions of language that Rene Daumal deemed Rasa. An American Book Award winner, he is the author of over twenty books across multiple genres. He is currently putting together a new book of plays.

STEVEN ALVAREZ is the author of *The Pocho Codex* and *The Xicano Genome*, both published by Editorial Paroxismo. He is assistant professor of writing, rhetoric, and digital studies at the University of Kentucky.

EMILY ANDERSON's writing has appeared in a variety of publications including *Harper's*, *Conjunctions*, *Fence*, and the *Kenyon Review*. Her first book, *Little:Novels*, is forthcoming from BlazeVox Books. Work from an ongoing collaboration with photo-video-based artist Jen Morris has been screened in Vermont, Philadelphia, and Spain. She holds an MFA from the School of the Art Institute of Chicago and is currently a PhD candidate in English at the University at Buffalo.

AARON APPS is the author of *Intersex* (Tarpaulin Sky Press, 2015) and *Dear Herculine*, winner of the 2014 Sawtooth Poetry Prize from Ahsahta Press. He is currently a doctoral student in English literature at Brown University. His writing has appeared in numerous journals, including *Pleiades*, *LIT*, *Washington Square Review*, *Puerto del Sol*, *Columbia Poetry Review*, and *Blackbird*.

DODIE BELLAMY's latest books are *The TV Sutras* (Ugly Duckling) and *Cunt Norton* (Les Figues). Her chapbook *Barf Manifesto* was named best book of 2009 under thirty pages by *Time Out New York*. Her reflections on the Occupy Oakland movement, "The Beating of Our Hearts," was published by Semiotext(e) in conjunction with the 2014 Whitney Biennial. With Kevin Killian she is editing for Nightboat Books' *New Narrative: 1977–1997*. *When the Sick Rule the World*, her third collection of essays, is forthcoming from Semiotext(e).

ANSELM BERRIGAN's recent books and chapbooks of poetry include *Pregrets* (Vagabond Press dB, 2014), *Loading*, a collaborative book with visual artist Jonathan Allen (Brooklyn Arts Press, 2013), *Sure Shot* (Overpass, 2013), and *Skasers*, with poet John Coletti (Flowers & Cream, 2012). He has published four books with Edge Books, most recently *Primitive State*, and a book-length poem, *Notes from Irrelevance*, with Wave Books. Wave will be publishing *Come In Alone* in 2016, which will include the poem found in this anthology and will be entirely made of poems in the same form.

JEREMY BLACHMAN is a freelance writer and the author of *Anonymous Lawyer* (Henry Holt), a novel satirizing the world of corporate law, developed for television by Sony and NBC and published in seven languages around the world. He is a graduate of Princeton University and Harvard Law School, and frequently writes short humor for the *Barnes and Noble Review*, *McSweeney's Internet Tendency*, and other publications. He lives in New York with his wife and son. Find him on Twitter @jeremyblachman or at jeremyblachman.com.

SHANE BOOK is a poet and filmmaker. He was educated at New York University, the Iowa Writers' Workshop, and Stanford, where he was a Stegner Fellow. His first collection, *Ceiling of Sticks* (University of Nebraska Press, 2010), won the Prairie Schooner Book Prize and the Great Lakes Colleges Association New Writers Award. His second collection, *Congotronic* (University of Iowa Press/House of Anansi Press, 2014) was a Kuhl House Poets Series Selection. Other honors include a *New York Times* fellowship, fellowships to the Telluride Film Festival and Flaherty Film Seminars, and a National Magazine Award. His latest film, *Praise and Blame*, was released in 2015.

CM BURROUGHS serves as assistant professor of poetry at Columbia College Chicago. Her debut collection of poetry, *The Vital System*, is available from Tupelo Press. Burroughs has been awarded fellowships and grants from Yaddo, the MacDowell Colony, Virginia Center for the Creative Arts, Cave Canem Foundation, Callaloo Writers Workshop, and the University of Pittsburgh. She has received commissions from the Studio Museum of Harlem and the Warhol Museum to create poetry in response to art installations. Her poetry has appeared in journals including *Callaloo*, *jubilat*, *Ploughshares*, *Volt*, *Bat City Review*, and *Sou'wester*. Burroughs is a graduate of Sweet Briar College and the MFA program at the University of Pittsburgh.

RACHEL CANTOR is the author of the novel *A Highly Unlikely Scenario* (Melville House, 2014) and the tentatively titled *Door Number Two* (Melville House, 2016). She has published more than two dozen stories in the *Paris Review*, *One Story*, *Kenyon Review*, *Ninth Letter*, *Fence*, *New England Review*, and elsewhere, and has three times been nominated for a Pushcart Prize. "Everyone's a Poet" is from her work in progress, a novel in stories about the Brontë siblings. She lives in Brooklyn.

XAVIER CAVAZOS is the author of *Barbarian at the Gate*, selected and introduced by Thomas Sayers Ellis as part of the Poetry Society of America's New American Poets Chapbook Series and *Diamond Grove Slave Tree*, the inaugural Prairie Seed Poetry Prize from Ice Cube Press. Cavazos teaches in the Central Washington Writing Project, Africana and Black Studies, and the Professional and Creative Writing Programs at Central Washington University.

CHING-IN CHEN is author of *The Heart's Traffic* and co-editor of *The Revolution Starts at Home: Confronting Intimate Violence Within Activist Communities*. A Kundiman, Lambda and Callaloo Fellow, they are part of Macondo and Voices of Our Nations Arts Foundation writing communities, and was a participant in Sharon Bridgforth's Theatrical Jazz Institute. They have been awarded fellowships and residencies from Can Serrat, Soul Mountain Retreat, Ragdale Foundation, Virginia Center for the Creative Arts, Millay Colony, and the Norman Mailer Center. They are *cream city review*'s editor-in-chief, senior editor of *The Conversant*, and serve on the board of Woodland Pattern. www.chinginchen.com.

CODY-ROSE CLEVIDENCE's first book, *Beast Feast*, was published by Ahsahta Press in 2014. They live in the Arkansas Ozarks with their dog, Pearl.

CECILIA CORRIGAN has been published in *Bomb*, *Capilano Review*, *Poetry Project Newsletter*, *Third Rail*, *Adult Magazine*, and *Prelude Magazine*, among other places. Her work has been reviewed in the *Chicago Review of Books*, *Chicago Tribune*, and *Poetry Project Newsletter*. *Titanic* (Northwestern University Press, 2014) was awarded the Madeleine P. Plonsker Prize for a first book, and appeared on two of Flavorwire's Books of the Year lists for 2014, for academic press and poetry titles. She has previously worked on HBO's *Luck*, for show-runner David Milch, and recently completed her first feature screenplay. In addition to writing for television, film, and theater, she has published fiction in *n+1* and elsewhere, and performs standup comedy. She has performed her work at MoMA, the New Museum, and Yale, Harvard, and Brown, and was most recently commissioned by the New York Performing Arts Collective.

SANTINO DELA is a visual artist who functions as myth, metaphor, and sometimes human being. He happens to exist in the spaces between words and beneath silences as they give shape to thoughts. The *New Yorker* has referred to his writing as "beautiful," and his work has been featured both online and in print by a number of different publishers, including Steve Roggenbuck's Boost House. Santino is deeply committed to his work and views it as a vehicle through which he can explore his own personal narrative as well as cultural archetypes and antagonisms. Language is his battleground, and he uses words like weapons in an attempt to provoke thought and induce sudden realizations. His examinations of modernity, absurdity, appropriation and authenticity explore what it means to be an individual in the twenty-first century. His examinations of the familiar are meant to induce a state in which ordinary reality suddenly seems imbued with a limitless matrix of extraordinary possibility. You can reach him online at santinodela.com.

DARCIE DENNIGAN is the author of three full-length poetry collections: *Corinna A-Maying the Apocalypse*, *Madame X*, and forthcoming in 2016, *Palace of Subatomic Bliss*. She works as the founder and co-director of Frequency Writers, a nonprofit arts organization in Providence, Rhode Island, and as a poet in residence at UConn. With artist Carl Dimitri, she created, in 2012, AGE OF AQUARIUS RISORGIMENTO whose most recent project is *Smoking Glue Gun's Dandelion Farm*.

STEVE DICKISON, poet, writer, and arts organizer, is director of the Poetry Center at San Francisco State University; he teaches there, and also at California College of the Arts. Recent writings appear in print publications *BOMB*, *Hambone*, *Aufgabe*, *Mandorla*, *Vanitas*, *Amerarcana*, *Where Eagles Dare*, and online at *EOAGH*, *ONandOnScreen*, and *Evening Will Come* (*The Volta*). Four poems from *Wear You to the Ball* received the 2014 BOMB Poetry

Prize, selected by CAConrad. *Sound Studio 3* (*Liner Notes*) was published by [2nd floor projects], and *Disposed* by the Post-Apollo Press. He lives in San Francisco.

KELLY DULANEY began in the deserts of Arizona; now, she lives and works in Denver, Colorado. She earned her MFA from the University of Colorado–Boulder and is co-editor of *The Cupboard Pamphlet*. Her work has appeared in *A-Minor Magazine*, *Springgun*, *Titmouse*, *Caketrain*, *Abjective*, and the *Albion Review*. Her novella *Ash* is forthcoming from Urban Farmhouse Press in 2015.

ANDREW DURBIN is the author of *Mature Themes* (Nightboat Books, 2014). He is a contributing editor of *Mousse*, co-edits Wonder, and lives in New York.

THOMAS SAYERS ELLIS, a photographer and poet, is the author of *The Maverick Room* and *Skin, Inc., Identity Repair Poems* (both from Graywolf Press). In 2014, he co-founded Heroes Are Gang Leaders, a group of poets and musicians, and recorded "The Amiri Baraka Sessions." His recent work has appeared in *PLUCK!*, *Best American Poetry 2015*, *Tin House*, *Paris Review*, *The Break beat Poets: New American Poetry in the Age of Hip Hop*, and *Poetry*. In 2015 he was the Richard Hugo Visiting Writer at the University of Montana and the Sterling A. Brown Professor of Humanities at Howard University.

BRYCE EMLEY is a freelance writer and MFA student at NC State University. His work can be found in the *Normal School*, *Mid-American Review*, *Prairie Schooner*, *Your Impossible Voice*, and others. He's on staff for *Raleigh Review* and *BULL: Men's Fiction*, and blogs about advertising at advertventures.wordpress.com.

ADAM FITZGERALD is the author of *The Late Parade* (2013), his debut collection of poems from W. W. Norton / Liveright. He is poetry editor for Literary Hub as well as founding editor of the online poetry journal *Maggy*. His poetry has appeared in the *New Yorker*, *Boston Review*, *Poetry*, *American Poetry Review*, *Granta* and elsewhere. An adjunct professor in creative writing at Rutgers University and NYU, he also directs The Home School (thehomeschool.org). His next book of poems, *George Washington*, is forthcoming in the fall of 2016.

SESSHU FOSTER has taught in East Los Angeles for thirty years. He's also taught writing at the University of Iowa, California Institute for the Arts, Naropa University's Jack Kerouac School of Disembodied Poetics, and the University of California–Santa Cruz. His work has been published in the Oxford *Anthology of Modern American Poetry*, *Language for a New Century: Poetry from the Middle East, Asia and Beyond*, and *State of the Union: 50 Political Poems*. Winner of two American Book Awards, his most recent books are the novel *Atomik Aztex* and the hybrid *World Ball Notebook*.

CARMEN GIMÉNEZ-SMITH is the author of a memoir and four poetry collections, including *Milk and Filth*, finalist for the 2013 NBCC award in poetry. A CantoMundo Fellow, she now teaches in the creative writing programs at New Mexico State University, while serving as editor-in-chief of the literary journal *Puerto del Sol* and publisher of Noemi Press.

C. S. GISCOMBE's poetry books include *Prairie Style*, *Giscome Road*, and *Here*; his book of linked essays (concerning Canada, race, and family) is *Into and Out of Dislocation*. His recognitions include the 2010 Stephen Henderson Award, an American Book Award (for *Prairie Style*), and the Carl Sandburg Prize (for *Giscome Road*). *Ohio Railroads* (a poem in essay form) was published in 2014, and *Border Towns* (essays on poetry, color, nature, television, and other topics) will appear in 2015. He teaches at the University of California–Berkeley. He is a long-distance cyclist.

RENEE GLADMAN's writings and drawings explore language and narration as architectures. Her most recent publication is *Ana Patova Crosses a Bridge* (Dororthy Project, 2013), which is the third installment of the Ravicka novella series. A collection of essays, *Calamities*, and a short novel, *Morelia*, are forthcoming in 2015. She lives in Providence, Rhode Island, and is a 2014–2015 Radcliffe Fellow at Harvard University.

MAGGIE GLOVER and ISAAC PRESSNELL received their MFAs in poetry from West Virginia University before going their separate ways in 2008, publishing extensively as individuals before reuniting as writing partners. The poem that appears here is an excerpt from their first collaborative manuscript, *YOU ASKED WHY WE COULDN'T JUST WORK OUT AND BE HAPPY*

TOGETHER TO WHICH I SAID, which renegotiates their shared past through an intersubjective authorial voice.

ALEXIS PAULINE GUMBS is a queer black troublemaker, a black feminist love evangelist, and an afro-antillean grandchild living in Durham, North Carolina. Alexis is the author of several collections of poetry including *Ogbe Oyeku: Black Feminist Book of the Dead and Unborn, 101 Things That Are Not True About the Most Famous Black Women Alive*, and *Good Hair Gone Forever.* Alexis is founder of the Eternal Summer of the Black Feminist Mind, an intergalactic community school; and co-founder of the Mobile Homecoming Project, an experiential archive amplifying generations of black LGBTQ brilliance.

ELIZABETH HALL is a writer and musician living in Los Angeles. Her work has appeared in *Birkensnake, Black Warrior Review, Delirious Hem, LIT*, and elsewhere. Her chapbook, *Two Essays*, is forthcoming from eohippus labs in spring 2015.

BRECKEN HANCOCK's poetry, essays, interviews, and reviews have appeared in *Lemon Hound, The Globe and Mail, Hazlitt, Studies in Canadian Literature*, and on the site Canadian Women in the Literary Arts. Her first book of poems, *Broom Broom*, came out with Coach House Books in 2014. She lives in Ottawa, Ontario.

DURIEL E. HARRIS is co-founder of the Black Took Collective and editor of *Obsidian: Literature & Arts in the African Diaspora*. She is the author of *Drag, Amnesiac: Poems* and *Speleology* (video). Nominated for the Pushcart Prize, her recent writing appears in *Fifth Wednesday* and *Kweli*, as well as *The Force of What's Possible* and *The &Now Awards 3*. A poet, performance artist, and scholar, Harris is a member of Douglas Ewart & Inventions creative music ensemble and Call & Response—a dynamic of Black women in performance. Current projects include the sound compilation "Black Magic" and *Thingification*—a one-woman show.

ROBERTO HARRISON is the author of *Os* (subpress, 2006), *Counter Daemons* (Litmus Press, 2006), *bicycle* (Noemi Press, forthcoming 2015), *culebra* (Green

Lantern Press, forthcoming 2015), as well as many chapbooks. With Andrew Levy he published and edited *Crayon* magazine from 1997 to 2008. He lives in Milwaukee, Wisconsin, with his wife, the poet Brenda Cárdenas.

LILY HOANG is the author of four books, including *Changing*, recipient of a PEN Open Books Award. With Joshua Marie Wilkinson, she edited the anthology *The Force of What's Possible: Writers on the Avant-Garde and Accessibility*. She teaches in the MFA program at New Mexico State University, where she is associate department head. She is prose editor at *Puerto del Sol* and CNF editor at *Drunken Boat*.

CATHY PARK HONG's latest collection of poems is *Engine Empire*. She is associate professor at Sarah Lawrence College, and she lives in New York.

JILL JICHETTI is a writer and artist. She holds a master of arts from New York University's Gallatin School of Individualized Study, and has just completed the Master of Fine Arts in Writing program at the School of the Art Institute of Chicago. She has been a playwright, self-portrait artist, and installation artist. She frequently performs. Awards include the Excellence in the Arts Award in Writing from the Council on the Arts and Humanities for Staten Island.

AISHA SASHA JOHN is a poet and dance artist. Her publications include *THOU* (BookThug 2014) and *The Shining Material* (BookThug 2011). She lives in Toronto.

BLAIR JOHNSON received her MFA from Washington University in St. Louis, where she currently teaches. Until moving to the Midwest, she lived next to the mountains in Utah. Other work has appeared in *Boston Review* and is forthcoming in *Diagram*.

JANINE JOSEPH is the author of *Driving Without a License* (Alice James Books, 2016), winner of the Kundiman Poetry Prize. Her commissioned work for the Houston Grand Opera (HGOco) stage includes a libretto, *From My Mother's Mother*, and a song cycle, *"On This Muddy Water": Voices from the*

Houston Ship Channel. She holds an MFA from New York University and a PhD from the University of Houston. Janine lives in Ogden, Utah, where she is assistant professor of English at Weber State University. Learn more at www.janinejoseph.com.

BHANU KAPIL teaches through the monster—a poetics of bodily life, trauma, and healing—at Naropa University's Jack Kerouac School of Disembodied Poetics. She is the author of five full-length, durational works: *The Vertical Interrogation of Strangers* and *Humanimal: A Project for Future Children* (Kelsey Street Press); *Incubation: A Space for Monsters* (Leon Works); and *Schizophrene* and *Ban en Banlieue* (Nightboat Books). What is a book? How do you write a book that vanishes before it arrives? How do you teach creative writing in ways that let this book, a book to be, become something that was not imagined or predicted in advance? Is this a correct approach? "Monster Checklist" was a hastily written syllabus for a seminar called The Hybrid that appeared on Bhanu's widely read blog on daily creative practices and encounters of different kinds: Was Jack Kerouac A Punjabi?

RUTH ELLEN KOCHER is the author of six books including, most recently, *Ending in Planes* (Noemi Press, 2014); *Goodbye Lyric: The Gigans and Lovely Gun* (Sheep Meadow Press, 2014); and *domina Un/blued* (Tupelo Press, 2013), Dorset Prize winner and the 2014 PEN Open Book Award. Her poems have appeared in various anthologies, including *Angles of Ascent: A Norton Anthology of Contemporary African American Poets* and *Black Nature*. She is a contributing editor at *Poets & Writers Magazine* and professor of English in the Creative Writing Program at the University of Colorado.

AARON KUNIN is the author of *Cold Genius* (Fence, 2014) and four other books of poetry and prose. He lives in Los Angeles.

DAVID LAU is the author of *Virgil and the Mountain Cat: Poems* (UC Press) and a chapbook called *Bad Opposites* (Spect Books). A second full-length collection is forthcoming from Commune Editions/AK Press in 2016. His poems and essays have appeared in *Counterpunch*, *The American Reader*, *Los Angeles Review of Books*, and *A Public Space*, and he has been a frequent contributor to *Armed Cell.* With Cal Bedient, he edits *Lana Turner: A Journal of Poetry and Opinion.* He teaches writing at the University of California–Santa Cruz and Cabrillo College.

SOPHIA LE FRAGA is a poet and artist. She is the author of *literallydead* (Spork Press, 2015); *I RL, YOU RL* (*Troll Thread* 2014; minutesBOOKS 2013); *I DON'T WANT ANYTHING TO DO WITH THE INTERNET* (Keep This Bag Away From Children, 2012), as well as the anti-plays *W8ING 4* and *TH3 B4LD 50PR4N0* (Gauss PDF, 2014). With Lanny Jordan Jackson, she co-authored *</V>*, an artist book about vape life. She is the poetry editor of *Imperial Matters* and on the poetry faculty at BHQFU.

SUEYEUN JULIETTE LEE grew up three miles from the CIA. A 2013 Pew Fellow in the Arts for Literature, her books include *That Gorgeous Feeling* (Coconut, 2008), *Underground National* (Factory School, 2011), and *Solar Maximum* (Futurepoem, 2015) as well as numerous chapbooks. She has held residencies at Kunstnarhuset Messen (Norway), Hafnarborg (Iceland), and UCross Foundation (Wyoming) for poetry and video art. She founded Corollary Press, a chapbook series dedicated to innovative multiethnic writing. She reviews contemporary poetry for the Constant Critic, a project of Fence Books, and has published essays on Asian American poetry and conceptual writing.

AMY LORRAINE LONG is a second-year MFA candidate in fiction at Virginia Tech. She holds a BA in English and women's studies and an MA in women's studies from the University of Florida. Amy previously worked in communications for drug policy reform and free speech advocacy groups in Santa Cruz, California; Washington, DC; and New York. She is a contributing editor to *Points: The Blog of the Alcohol and Drugs History Society.* Amy lives in Blacksburg, Virginia.

DAWN LUNDY MARTIN, an essayist and award-winning poet, is author of *A Gathering of Matter / A Matter of Gathering* (2007) and *DISCIPLINE* (Nightboat Books, 2011), which was selected by Fanny Howe for the Nightboat Books Poetry Prize and was a finalist for both the Los Angeles Times Book Prize and the Lambda Literary Award. Her most recent collection is *Life in a Box is a Pretty Life* (Nightboat Books, 2015). She wrote the libretto for a video installation opera, titled "Good Stock on the Dimension Floor," which was scheduled to be featured in the 2014 Whitney Biennial. Martin is also a co-founder of the Black Took Collective, an experimental performance art/poetry group of three, and a member of HOWDOYOUSAYYAMINAFRICAN? global arts collective. She is associate professor of English at the University of Pittsburgh.

JOYELLE MCSWEENEY is the author of numerous books of poetry and prose, most recently *Salamandrine* and *8 Gothics* (Tarpaulin Sky), *Percussion Grenade* (Fence), and *Dead Youth, or, The Leaks* (Winner, Leslie Scalapino Prize for Innovative Women Playwrights; Litmus Press, 2014). She is also the author of the critical work *The Necropastoral: Poetry, Media, Occults*, published in 2015 by the University of Michigan Poets on Poetry Series. She edits Action Books and is director of the Creative Writing Program at Notre Dame.

HOLLY MELGARD is the author of several books of poetry: the *Poems for Baby* trilogy (2011), *The Making of The Americans* (2012), *Black Friday* (2012), *Reimbursement* (2013), and *Working, Making, Talking* (Company Books, forthcoming). She currently co-edits Troll Thread Press, teaches composition, and writes her PhD dissertation as part of the Buffalo Poetics Program. She lives in Brooklyn, New York.

TYLER MILLS is the author of *Tongue Lyre*, winner of the 2011 Crab Orchard Series in Poetry First Book Award (SIU Press, 2013). Her poems have recently appeared in *Believer*, *Blackbird*, *Boston Review*, and *Poetry*. She earned a PhD in poetry from the University of Illinois–Chicago.

ELENA MINOR is the author of *TITULADA* (Noemi Press, 2014). Her work has been published in more than two dozen literary journals, including *Jacket2, MAKE, Hot Metal Bridge, RHINO, Puerto del Sol, Switchback, Mandorla*, and *Shadowbox*, and is included in *Angels of the Americlypse*, an anthology of new Latin@ writing, edited by Carmen Giménez Smith and John Chávez. She is a first prize recipient of the Chicano/Latino Literary Prize and founding editor of *PALABRA*.

NICK MONTFORT develops computational art and poetry, often collaboratively. He is on the faculty at MIT in comparative media studies/ writing and is the principal of the naming firm Nomnym. Montfort wrote the books of poems *#!* and *Riddle & Bind*, co-wrote *2002: A Palindrome Story*, and developed more than forty digital projects including the collaborations *The Deletionist* and *Sea and Spar Between*. The MIT Press has published four of his collaborative and individual books: *The New Media Reader, Twisty Little Passages, Racing the Beam*, and *10 PRINT CHR$(205.5+RND(1)); : GOTO 10*, with *Exploratory Programming for the Arts and Humanities* coming soon.

FRED MOTEN is author of *In the Break: The Aesthetics of the Black Radical Tradition, Hughson's Tavern, B. Jenkins, The Undercommons: Fugitive Planning and Black Study* (with Stefano Harney), *The Feel Trio*, and *The Little Edges*. He lives in Los Angeles and teaches at the University of California–Riverside.

DANIEL NADLER was born in Canada. He is an entrepreneur, and directs research at the Global Projects Center at Stanford University. A recent graduate of Harvard University, he divides his time between New York and Los Angeles.

SUNNY NAGRA is about to graduate from the University of California–Irvine and is currently terrified about his future (but in a cool, ironic, hip way, he pretends).

KELLY NELSON is the author of the chapbook *Rivers I Don't Live By* (Concrete Wolf, 2014). Her cross-language erasures have appeared in *RHINO, Jet Fuel Review, Quarter After Eight, Poetry WTF?!*, and *Mojave River Review*. She teaches interdisciplinary studies at Arizona State University.

MENDI + KEITH OBADIKE make music, art, and literature. They have four books: *Armor and Flesh: Poems* (Lotus Press), *Big House / Disclosure*—a book and CD (1913 Press), *Four Electric Ghosts* (1913 Press), and *Phonotype* (Ramapo)—a book and CD of media artworks. Their works also include *The Sour Thunder: An Internet Opera* (Bridge Records); *Crosstalk: American Speech Music*, an anthology of text sound works (Bridge Records); and Black.Net.Art Actions, a suite of new media artworks (published in re:skin on MIT Press).

Mendi + Keith were invited to develop *Four Electric Ghosts*, their first "opera-masquerade," by writer Toni Morrison at her Princeton Atelier. Their other honors include a Rockefeller New Media Arts Fellowship, Pick Laudati Award for Digital Art, a New York Foundation for the Arts Fellowship in Fiction, and a Vectors Fellowship from USC. They are currently completing a series of intermedia projects about America. The work presented in this collection comes from *Big House / Disclosure*, the first in the series.

LANCE OLSEN is the author of more than twenty books of and about innovative writing, including three published last year: the novel based on Robert Smithson's earthwork the Spiral Jetty, *Theories of Forgetting*; *How to Unfeel the Dead: New & Selected Fictions*; and *[[there.]]*, a trash-diary meditation on the confluence of travel, curiosity, and aesthetic/existential experimentation. A Guggenheim, Berlin Prize, Artist-in-Berlin Residency, NEA Fellowship, and Pushcart Prize recipient, as well as a Fulbright Scholar, he teaches experimental narrative theory and practice at the University of Utah and chairs the board of directors at the independent press Fiction Collective Two.

KIKI PETROSINO is the author of two poetry volumes: *Hymn for the Black Terrific* (2013) and *Fort Red Border* (2009), both from Sarabande Books. She is associate professor of English and director of creative writing at the University of Louisville.

JESSY RANDALL's poems, poetry comics, and diagram poems have appeared in *McSweeney's*, *Painted Bride Quarterly*, *Rattle*, and *West Wind*. Her most recent books are *Injecting Dreams into Cows* (Red Hen) and *There Was an Old Woman* (Unicorn). She is curator of special collections at Colorado College, and her website is personalwebs.coloradocollege.edu/~jrandall.

JACOB REBER is an artist and writer living in Columbus, Ohio, where he co-curates Hystericallyreal.com. His recent work has appeared or is forthcoming in *West Wind Review*, *PANK*, *Out of Nothing*, *KTBAFC*, and *BlazeVOX*. He is the author of *No Results* (LUMA/89plus) and *TAPE 181* (Gauss PDF).

J D SCOTT is the author of *Night Errands* (YellowJacket Press, 2012) and *FUNERALS & THRONES* (Birds of Lace Press, 2013). He lives in Tuscaloosa, Alabama.

EVIE SHOCKLEY is the author of *the new black* (Wesleyan, 2011; winner of the 2012 Hurston/Wright Legacy Award) and *a half-red sea* (Carolina Wren Press, 2006), both poetry collections, and the critical study *Renegade Poetics: Black Aesthetics and Formal Innovation in African American Poetry* (Iowa, 2011). Her work appears widely in journals and anthologies and has been awarded the Holmes National Poetry Prize and fellowships from ACLS and the Schomburg Center for Research in Black Culture, among other honors. She serves as creative writing editor for *Feminist Studies* and is associate professor of English at Rutgers University–New Brunswick.

BALTHAZAR SIMÕES writes letters and takes photographs. He was once an aspirant monk, but then chose other aspirations. He lives in Brooklyn, New York.

GIOVANNI SINGLETON's debut poetry collection, *Ascension* (Counterpath Press), informed by the music and life of Alice Coltrane, received the 81st California Book Award Gold Medal. She is founding editor of *nocturnes (re) view of the literary arts*, a journal dedicated to work of the African Diaspora and other contested spaces. Her work has been exhibited in the Smithsonian Institution's American Jazz Museum, San Francisco's first Visual Poetry and Performance Festival, and on the building of Yerba Buena Center for the Arts.

BRIAN KIM STEFANS teaches new media studies and twentieth-/twenty-first-century American poetry in the English department at UCLA. He is the author of several books of poetry including "*Viva Miscegenation*" (MakeNow, 2014) and *What is Said to the Poet Concerning Flowers* (Heretical Texts, 2006). A collection of essays, *Word Toys: Poetry and Technics*, is forthcoming in 2016 from University of Alabama Press. His digital texts, videos, and other miscellaneous items can be viewed on arras.net.

READ NAT SUFRIN's recent work in the *Antioch Review*, *InDigest*, and *BlazeVOX*. Say hi if you're in Chicago.

VINCENT TORO has an MFA in poetry from Rutgers University. He is a Pushcart Prize nominee and finalist for the Alice James Book Award and the Andres Montoya Poetry Prize. Vincent is recipient of a 2014 Poet's House Emerging Poets Fellowship and a New York Foundation for the Arts Fellowship in Poetry. His poems have been published in *Rattapallax*, *Vallum*, *Bordersenses*, *Kweli*, *Buenos Aires Review*, *Acentos Review*, and *Codex*, and in the anthologies *CHORUS* and *The Waiting Room Reader 2*. He lives and teaches in the Bronx with his wife, writer and scholar Dr. Grisel Acosta.

RODRIGO TOSCANO's newest book of poetry is *Deck of Deeds* (Counterpath Press 2012). His previous collection, *Collapsible Poetics Theater*, was a 2007 National Poetry Series Selection. Forthcoming from Fence Books in 2016 is *Explosion Rocks Springfield*. He was the recipient of a New York State Fellowship in Poetry. His poetry has appeared in numerous anthologies, including *Against Expression*, *Diasporic Avant Gardes*, *Angels of the Americlypse*, and *Best American Poetry*. Toscano works for the Labor Institute in conjunction with the United Steelworkers and the National Institute for Environmental Health Science. He lives in the Greenpoint township of Brooklyn.

TOM TRUDGEON is a writer, editor, and curator from Los Angeles. He has been published in *Out Of Nothing*, *The Conversant*, *The Volta*, *Entropy*, Gauss PDF, and elsewhere. He co-edits the art book publication *Basic Editions*. He is a recent MFA graduate from Temple University where he currently teaches "experimental" poetry. His web site is tomtrudgeon.com.

SARAH VAP is the author of five collections of poetry and poetics. She is the recipient of a 2013 National Endowment of the Arts Grant for Literature, and her sixth collection, *Viability*, was selected for the National Poetry Series prize and is forthcoming from Penguin (2015).

DIVYA VICTOR is the author of *Natural Subjects* (Trembling Pillow, 2014; winner of the Bob Kaufman Award), *UNSUB* (Insert Blanc, 2015), *Things to Do With Your Mouth* (Les Figues, 2014), *Swift Taxidermies 1919–1922* (Gauss PDF, 2014), *Goodbye John! On John Baldessari* (Gauss PDF, 2012), *PUNCH* (Gauss PDF, 2011), and the Partial Trilogy (*Troll Thread*, 2011–2012). She lives in the United States and Singapore.

KIM VODICKA is the author of *Aesthesia Balderdash* (Trembling Pillow Press, 2012). She holds an MFA in creative writing from Louisiana State University (2013). Her poems, art, and other writings have been published in or are forthcoming from *Shampoo, Ekleksographia, Spork, Unlikely Stories, RealPoetik, Cloudheavy Zine, THEthe Poetry, Finery, Women Poets Wearing Sweatpants, Epiphany, Industrial Lunch, Moss Trill, Smoking Glue Gun, Luna Luna, Paper Darts, The Gambler, The Volta, Deluge, glitterMOB, Tarpaulin Sky, Queen Mob's Teahouse*, and *The Electric Gurlesque*. Cruise more of her work at ih8kimvodicka.tumblr.com.

CATHERINE WAGNER's collections of poetry include *Nervous Device* (City Lights, 2012) as well as *My New Job, Macular Hole*, and *Miss America* (all from Fence). Some of her readings and songs can be heard on PennSound. Her interests include civil rights and labor activism. She is professor in the creative writing program at Miami University in Oxford, Ohio, where she lives with her son.

TYRONE WILLIAMS is the author of five books and several chapbooks of poetry, including *Red Between Green* (2014). He is also the author of a prose eulogy, *Pink Tie.*

RONALDO V. WILSON, PhD, is the author of *Narrative of the Life of the Brown Boy and the White Man* (University of Pittsburgh, 2008), winner of the 2007 Cave Canem Poetry Prize; *Poems of the Black Object* (Futurepoem Books, 2009), winner of the Thom Gunn Award and the Asian American Literary Award in Poetry in 2010; and the forthcoming collections *Farther Traveler: Poetry, Prose, Other* (Counterpath Press, 2015) and *Lucy 72* (1913 Press, 2015). Co-founder of the Black Took Collective, Wilson is assistant professor of poetry, fiction and literature in the literature department at the University of California–Santa Cruz.

STEVEN ZULTANSKI is the author of *Bribery* (Ugly Duckling Presse, 2014), *Agony* (BookThug, 2012), *Cop Kisser* (BookThug, 2010), and *Pad* (Make Now, 2010).